Sham Ruins

In the middle of the eighteenth century, a new fad found its way into the gardens of England's well-to-do: building fake Gothic ruins. Newly constructed castle towers and walls looked like they were already falling apart, even on the first day of their creation. Made of stone, plaster, or even canvas, these "sham ruins" are often considered an embarrassing blip in English architectural history. However, *Sham Ruins: A User's Guide* expands the specific example of the sham ruin into a general principle to examine the way purposely broken objects can be used to both uncover old truths and invent new ones. Along with architecture, work by Ivan Vladislavić, Tom Stoppard, Alain Mabanckou, Aleksei Fedorchenko, Michael Haneke, and Sturtevant is used to develop this thesis, as well as artifacts such as pre-torn jeans, fake histories, and broken screen apps. Using these examples, one of the key questions the book raises is: what is it that sham ruins ruin? In other words, if real ruins are ruins of what they actually are, then sham ruins should be considered ruins of what they are not. Thus, sham ruins are about imposing new meaning where such meaning does not and should not exist. They also can show how things we think are functioning well are actually already broken. Sham ruins do this, and much more, by being lies, ruses, and embarrassments. This is what gives them the power with which we can think about objects in new, unintended ways.

Brian Willems is Associate Professor of Literature and Film Theory at the University of Split, Croatia. He is most recently the author of *Speculative Realism and Science Fiction* (2017) and *Shooting the Moon* (2015). He has curated exhibitions of new media art in Croatia and Slovenia and is the author of the novella *Henry, Henry* (2017).

Routledge Focus on Literature

For more information about this series, please visit: www.routledge.com/
Routledge-Focus-on-Literature/book-series/RFLT

Sham Ruins
A User's Guide

Brian Willems

NEW YORK AND LONDON

First published 2022
by Routledge
605 Third Avenue, New York, NY 10158

and by Routledge
2 Park Square, Milton Park, Abingdon, Oxon, OX14 4RN

Routledge is an imprint of the Taylor & Francis Group, an informa business

Library of Congress Cataloging-in-Publication Data
A catalog record for this book has been requested

ISBN: 978-1-032-08131-1 (hbk)
ISBN: 978-1-032-08135-9 (pbk)
ISBN: 978-1-003-21308-6 (ebk)

DOI: 10.4324/9781003213086

Typeset in Times New Roman
by Apex CoVantage, LLC

To Jasna

Contents

Acknowledgments

Thank you to Sherryl Vint, Laurence Rickels, Steven Shaviro, Mark Bould, James Graham, Miguel Llansó, and Levi Bryant for the encouragement. I am grateful for all the kindness and focus from those at Routledge, including Emily Briggs, Michelle Salyga, and Bryony Reece. The text is much better because of them. Part of the research for this book was kindly provided by a grant from the Faculty of Humanities and Social Sciences, University of Split, for a trip to the British Library in 2016. Further assistance came from the project *Further development of Centre for Cross-Cultural and Korean Studies at the University of Split* (Project 20180060). Portions of the text have previously appeared, in slightly different forms, as the following: Brian Willems, "The Potential of the Past: *First on the Moon*," *Science Fiction Film and Television*, Vol. 9, No. 2 (2016): 159–179 and Brian Willems, "Punked Objects: Salvagepunk in *Perdido Street Station* and *Crumbs*," *Deletion*, No. 14 (2018).[1] I would like to thank the editors of these journals for permission to reprint the material here.

Note

1. Internet: www.deletionscifi.org/episodes/episode-14/punked-objects-salvagepunk-in-perdido-street-station-and-crumbs/.

Preface

Sham Ruins: A User's Guide features purposely broken objects in architecture, literature, films, and art. The thesis of the book is that sabotaging the correlation between the purpose of an object and its actual behavior can lead to change. However, this is not a book about do-it-yourself (DYI) repurposing. Nor is it a re-reading of something like Joseph Schumpeter's free-market concept of "creative destruction." Rather, the book focuses on objects that were never meant to function as expected, things that were 'born broken' and thus have an odd functionality, to begin with. Pre-torn jeans, fake histories, replicated artwork, and broken screen apps are all read as fake ruins that fall under this category.

In eighteenth-century England, a new craze swept the fancy gardens of the rich and bored, building fake Gothic ruins in order to enhance the look and feel of their estates. These were towers which crumbled on their very first day, walls which were never meant to reach their full height, and staircases that lead to nowhere. Made of stone, plaster, and sometimes even canvas, such 'sham ruins' were never taken seriously and caused the ire of many. This book attempts to take these merely decorative objects and see how their playfulness can actually make objects function in unintended ways, at times even showing how objects, where taken to be fully functional, were really shams all along.

Thus, *Sham Ruins: A User's Guide* expands the specific example of the sham ruin into a general principle to examine the way purposely ruined objects can be used to both uncover old truths and invent new ones. Some of the work that it examines includes Ivan Vladislavić's novel *The Folly* (1993), Tom Stoppard's play *Arcadia* (1993), Alain Mabanckou's novel *Black Moses* (2017), Aleksei Fedorchenko's film *Pervye na Lune/First on the Moon* (2005), Michael Haneke's film *The Seventh Continent* (1989), and Sturtevant's replications of famous, male-made, artwork.

One of the key questions the book raises is: what do sham ruins actually ruin? They are not 'real' ruins. Real ruins are ruins of an actual object: if you go visit the ruins of Pompeii, this is because you want to see the destruction of something 'real' that existed in a different form before 79 AD and that was ruined after. Sham ruins are different. There is nothing 'real' behind them in time. Sham ruins are not ruins of something that was, but rather of something that was not. Sham ruins are about representing what is unrepresented. They are about creating new meaning where such meaning does not and should not exist. Sham ruins are jokes, games, decorations, and embarrassments. And this is what gives them the force with which we can think about objects in new, unintended ways.

The first chapter of the book looks at the aesthetic and political uses of sham ruins from architectural, historic, and literary perspectives. From sixteenth-century sham ruins described by Giorgio Vasari to the eighteenth-century fad in the Gothic Revival, sham ruins are taken as objects whose flimsy aesthetic appeal hides a manner for interrogating the past. Even more importantly, they function as objects of sabotage because over time, sham ruins become indistinguishable from real ones. Using Graham Harman's concept of "ruination" and Evan Calder Williams' reading of "hostile objects," Tom Stoppard's play *Arcadia*, which takes place inside a sham ruin, is reconfigured into a theoretical text about the historical function of such ruins. Once these different objects are all gathered together under the common term of 'sham ruins,' some of the truths that they ruin becomes apparent. One thing that contemporary sham ruins seem to be doing is attacking user-friendliness. Although there are huge open source and DYI communities out there, most of the objects we use are closed off behind single buttons and warranty-invalidating contract agreements. Breaking these objects is a way of making them do things they are not meant to do, even if that new thing is simply not to work. This is not an example of something like Mark Granovetter's concept of *weak ties*. Rather, contemporary sham ruins are objects of political sabotage, not in the sense of critiquing a specific ideology, but by claiming new uses for old objects.

In the second chapter, a key feature of sham ruins is developed: their relationship to the past and the present. Aleksei Fedorchenko's film *Pervye na Lune/First on the Moon* suggests that alternative histories are not about militarism or extreme dystopias. The film purports to be a documentary showing that Russia landed on the moon in the 1930s, long before the Americans. Yet the film is less a skewed reflection of current woes than a mediation on the relationship between the past and possibility. In other words, if alternative histories are derided as shams for eschewing the more traditional view of science fiction which sees change located in the future, *First on the Moon* suggests that the future is locked down, meaning that the limitless possibilities of what-is-to-come have already been decided for us. Reflecting the thought of Paolo Virno and Graham Harman, and looking at a video artwork by Pierre Huyghe, the chapter paradoxically suggests that it is positing history as a sham ruin which creates alternatives to the present. In fact, this idea will be taken one step further: *First on the Moon* shows that potentiality is only located in the past and never in the future.

The third chapter looks at a number of contemporary examples of sham ruins in order to challenge user-friendliness. Breaking objects is a way of making them do things they are not meant to do, even if that new thing is simply not to work. The chapter begins with a reading of Erasmus' *The Praise of Folly*, in which Folly describes how some lies are easy to spot while others are not. This initial division is used to discuss a number of art-works, such as a 'broken' Brâncuşi sculpture at Harlem's Studio Museum, an all-white chessboard by Yoko Ono, and re-touched photos of real ruins removed from the *New York Times* website. These new sham ruins are polit-ical not in the sense of critiquing a specific way of thinking but rather in showing how some objects always functioned differently than it was gener-ally perceived. The way this is done is by breaking new objects in a myriad of different ways. This leads to the main example of the chapter. In the 1960s, the American artist Sturtevant began testing the connection between change and the fake when she started making replications of famous, mainly male-made, artwork, sometimes even using the same techniques as the orig-inal artists – Warhol's actual printing screens and Jasper Johns' hot wax painting technique for her version of the latter's flag paintings, for example. Yet she was not making forgeries, since these copies were shown using her own name. Instead, her art aimed at the "total structure" of work she was replicating, thus sabotaging not only the assumed connections between the market, museums, work, and gender but also the whole art world that makes such connections possible. To develop this argument, Graham Harman's idea of "self-contained objects" and Levi Bryant's reading of the end of the world is key since they help in the understanding that all the work in this chapter aims to disrupt value before the mechanisms of the market come into play, thus functioning as objects broken from their inception.

In the final chapter, Alain Mabanckou's novel *Black Moses* is used to show how every home is already a sham ruin. When the titular character loses his home, he also loses his mind in the sense that he can no lon-ger utilize the grammatical category of the adverbial. This event is then used to show how a number of films feature the destruction of a home – Francis Ford Coppola's *The Conversation* (1974), Michael Haneke's *The Seventh Continent*, and Jean-Marc Vallée's *Demolition* (2015), all do so in order to show how the home was already malfunctioning from the begin-ning. In order to support this thesis, the idea of 'punking objects' is pro-posed. Looking at China Miéville's novel *Perdido Street Station* (2000) and Miguel Llansó's film *Crumbs* (2015), the idea of showing the way that objects are dysfunctional, from the very beginning, is proposed. The chapter then ends with a reading of Ivan Vladislavić's novel *The Folly*, which features a home built as a sham ruin from the very beginning, and which was the original inspiration for this project.

Through all these examples, and many more, sham ruins, one of the most useless architectural features, are given, in a rather tongue-in-cheek manner, a user's guide. Yet there is a serious side to this argument also, since in an age when the function of the objects around us is already streamlined under the guise of user-friendliness, almost any strategy for making our own way in the world should be welcome.

1   Not Just Ruins

In the 1740s England, a new fad found its way into the gardens of the well-to-do: building fake Gothic ruins. Newly constructed castle towers and walls looked like they were already falling apart, even on the first day of their creation. Made of stone, plaster, or even canvas, these 'sham ruins' are often taken as an embarrassing blip in English architectural history. However, their reevaluation can help in identifying the sham ruins of our own age, as well as in understanding what makes a freshly minted broken object a potent fulcrum for change.

The person at the helm of this art of the fake in England was gentleman architect Sanderson Miller. In the mid-1740s, he started building the sham ruin that solidified the craze, at his family estate, Radway Grange at Edgehill, Warwickshire. It includes an octagonal tower with windows too big to deflect enemy arrows, and crumbling walls so weak they could only help defend against the most tepid of foes. Now it is a pub called the Castle Inn with its own Facebook page.

Miller's sham was supposed to be appreciated more than used. As such, it is a prime example of Gothic Revival architecture in England. As art historian Kenneth Clark says of the period, the Gothic Revival aimed "to stimulate the imagination" (46–7) and nothing more. At the same time, such sham structures were not to everyone's liking. John Ruskin's take on the period was that "I know nothing in the shape of error so dark as this, no imbecility so absolute, no treachery so contemptible" (371). But figuring out why Miller made what he did and what it was supposed to mean is not straightforward.

He built his structure on the spot that Charles I supposedly raised his standard and rallied his troops during the English Civil War. But the party he held for the official opening of the structure was on September 3, 1750, an anniversary of the death of Oliver Cromwell. These two dates indicate the difficulty in interpreting this sham ruin. Is it a tribute to Charles I, a Catholic sympathizer, or built-in honor of Cromwell, a radical Puritan who

DOI: 10.4324/9781003213086-1

was one of the signatories of Charles I's death warrant? Are sham ruins just a pretty decoration, part of a picturesque landscape? Or are they meant to illustrate how the original Gothic buildings of England's Catholic past were not strong enough to last? Are they merely pretty ornaments, or political symbols built in support of the Jacobite rebellion of 1745? According to Lauren Kaplan, it depends on which sham ruin you look at (Kaplan).

Miller's first sham ruin at Edgehill seems to lie somewhere between a purely aesthetic object and a political statement, a fact belied by the contradictory dates found at its inception and inauguration (63–4). Another construction of Miller's at Hagley Hall is more clearly polemical. It was commissioned by patron of the arts George Lyttleton (to whom Henry Fielding's *Tom Jones* is dedicated). Lyttleton was a well-known critic of the original Gothic period of England. Thus, he saw his ruins functioning as what David Stewart calls "images of *just* destruction" (400), meaning that ruined medieval towers were ways of showing how the dark ages of Catholicism were not strong enough to survive in the present age of reason.

In another example, an intended political effect was eventually watered down. Lord Hardwick, who saw the sham ruins at Hagley Hall and admired their political portent, hired Miller to create something similar for his own estate. Yet due to Miller's issues with mental health, which began in the 1770s (Headley and Meulenkamp 141), the work was only completed after Miller's death in 1780. Left to the Hardwick family's own architect, the political construction was prettified into a merely picturesque garden accessory.

What becomes apparent is that a fair amount of background knowledge is necessary in order to understand the context of this rather trite object. Kaplan foregrounds this fact by arguing that for the twenty-first-century viewers, sham ruins are simply "exotic" in the sense that they are not firmly rooted in the past, because they are fake, but they are also not located in the present, because the context of their production is generally lost to the average viewer (56–7). Thus, sham ruins become objects lost in time, holding no real meaning except to generate a sense of wonder about what strange creatures they are.

On the other hand, contemporary viewers of sham ruins have sometimes subsumed them into thought on ruins in general. Thus, the way that real ruins confuse the clear separation of inside and outside, foreground processes of decay, engender a nostalgia for the past, or contrast the sterile present with a feral history is considered equally applicable to the fake ruins that mock them.

However, in order to make the separation between sham ruins and real ones a bit clearer, a simple question can be asked: what is it that sham ruins ruin? In other words, if real ruins are ruins of what they actually are, meaning that the ruins of the Acropolis are a real ruined Acropolis, then perhaps sham ruins should be considered ruins of what they are not. It is this fundamental insight which will inform much of the thought in this book. Sham ruins are about representing what is unrepresented. They are about imposing new meaning where such meaning does not and should not exist. Real ruins represent the decay of real objects. The decay of sham ruins is fake, at least when they are first constructed. Sham ruins are lies, ruses, and embarrassments. And this is what gives them their power as objects with which to think about using things in new, unintended ways.

Early Sham Ruins

The first example of a sham ruin is usually taken to be one built around 1510 by Girolamo Genga for the garden of the Duke of Urbino's Pesaro Palace in Venice. It included a staircase supposedly copied from one in the Belvedere Court of the Vatican. It is known through a description in Giorgio Vasari's *Lives of the Painters, Sculptors, and Architects*: "The Duke caused the Palace at Pesaro to be restored, and also the little park, making within it a house representing a ruin, which is a very beautiful thing to see" (Vasari 2:384–5).

Rose Macaulay, in her classic book on ruins from the 1950s called *Pleasure of Ruins*, comments on how many more sham ruins like the one at Pesaro Palace were built. Her comment then addresses one thing that sham ruins ruin: they ruin time.

> How many more of these were there? They were not written about, gossiped about, written up, as the later follies were; they took their places quietly, decorating gardens and landscapes with broken arches and columns, believed, no doubt, by later generations to have fallen into ruin. How can one tell? Increasingly, ruin assumed its place as the romantic background, the foil to the practical bustle of living, the broken arch through which a distant vista showed, stretching into infinity, stretching back to the long dim reaches of the past.
>
> (16)

Macaulay highlights the way sham ruins become indiscernible from actual ruins over time. Both kinds of ruin stand next to each other as equals. When this happens, the passage of time that real ruins record can no longer be trusted. In this way, time is ruined by sham ruins.[1]

In other words, it is not so much that, as William Viney argues, "Making and marking time . . . forms a crucial component in the building of ruinous follies and folly gardens" (146). Rather, sham ruins disrupt time, instead of merely marking it. And while for Kaplan the exoticness of sham ruins removes any political dimension from their understanding, Macaulay designates an even more fundamental disruption: they make historical evidence untrustworthy. Interest in ruins as historical evidence started in fifteenth-century Italy, with Flavio Biondo's *Rome Restored* (1444–8) and *Triumphant Rome* (1479) (Breisach 156). The untrustworthy effect of sham ruins, on the other hand, reaches out into the past, unsettling knowledge about the ruins that came before, and of those out into the future, invalidating the real ruins to come. The real number of sham ruins will always be unknown. However, this is true not only for the sixteenth century but also for the sham ruins of our own time. The patina of antiques and the wear-and-tear of originals can too easily be faked. However, ruse is not the only function of the sham ruin.

In the seventeenth century, another Roman sham ruin was built. The aim was presumably to fit new architecture into the ruins of the old buildings surrounding it (Bratton 100). The Italian architect and creator of the baroque style of sculpture, Gian Lorenzo Bernini, built a bridge with an intentionally absent keystone at the Palazzo Barberini in Rome, where it can still be seen. Called the *Ponte Ruinante* (or 'falling bridge'), Bernini's work was a functioning bridge, providing access to the upper area of the Palazzo's gardens. Its ruined aspect was mere appearance.

Both these Roman sham ruins were formed out of a similar intention: to blend in. Located in the heart of Rome, these fake ruins were constructed amid real ones. They were meant to match their surroundings, and as Macaulay describes it, many sham ruins of the time have actually now become completely indistinguishable from their genuinely crumbling surroundings.

However, the sham ruins which are the focus of this study are different. Rather than fitting into their surroundings, they stand out from them. Sham ruins are not majestic players in the eternal city; rather, they are embarrassing hemorrhages littering the backyards of people with too much money and too little taste. They are ugly, flimsy, and utterly useless. Sham ruins feature "Towers that no one ever climbed, turrets that no one could enter, and battlements that no one rose to defend" (Mumford 78). Sham ruins impede serious thought. They are signs of a complete lack of culture. This is as true for the sham ruins of England as those of Ireland (Howley), France (Robinson), Canada (McAleer), and California (Perusse).

The Exform, and Not

The way that sham ruins can be both political and uselessly aesthetic finds a somewhat cloudy mirror in what Nicolas Bourriaud calls "the exform," meaning "the site where border negotiations would unfold between what is rejected and what is admitted, products and waste" (x). The discarded, excluded, and rejected make up the exform, which features "an authentically organic link between the aesthetic and the political" (ibid.). Bourriaud is interested in art made out of what is usually considered trash, whether that is the kitschy objects of Jeff Koons or the repurposed old newspapers and bottle caps of George Adéagbo or El Anatsui. Such marginalized and cast-off objects are of interest because they can be used to instigate change in two different ways. First, in order for a subject to change, something has to break (9). Second, in order to challenge a dominant system, "one must first conceive its nature as *precarious*" (36, emphasis in original). The exform, meaning art created from waste, fits into both strategies for change. Waste can consist of broken objects, and broken objects can be reminiscent of broken systems.

Therefore, Bourriaud conceives of the exform as waste, in other words, it is "what the process of production leaves behind" (97). This waste is then repurposed by artists into strategies for change. Sham ruins are both similar and different. They are similar because their broken nature can function as a fulcrum for change. However, they are different because they are not waste, meaning they are not the actual by-product of the production of something else. Rather than being objects of waste, sham ruins are new products which are purposely wasteful. They have not lost their function but were never meant to function, at least not as the buildings they represent. This difference gives sham ruins a strange power. They are not ruined objects, like waste, but rather objects which ruin.

This difference is seen in the way that eighteenth-century priest and theorist of the picturesque, William Gilpin, describes the difference in building a sham ruin in comparison to building a fully functioning building. For Gilpin, the sham ruin is much harder to build, because the construction of weakness is an art that few know:

> It is not every man who can build a house, that can execute a ruin. To give the stone its mouldering appearance, to make the widening chink run naturally through all the joints, to mutilate the ornaments, to peel the facing from the internal structure, to shew how correspondent parts have once united; though now the chasm runs wide between them, and to scatter heaps of ruin around with negligence and ease, are great efforts of art; much too delicate for the hand of a common workman; and what we very rarely see performed.
>
> (67–8)

Yet the hand of an artist is not enough for the completion of the sham ruin. The work needs to be completed by nature (68), which eventually leads the ruin to become a part of nature, and thus to be potentially ruined itself (Dillon 59).

Gilpin sees nature as completing the aesthetic work of the ruin, and a prime example of the picturesque quality of all ruins (cf. Wölfflin 24). However, another aspect is added by keeping Macaulay's comments in mind. Macaulay argued that it is impossible to know all the sham ruins of the past because the real erosion of time has made them indistinguishable from real ruins (16). This is the active nature of sham ruins that is not contained in the idea of the exform: reaching out into the future in order to disrupt ideas of authenticity.

The future aspect of ruins has been noted before. As Brian Dillon has shown, Hubert Robert painted the future ruins of the Louvre in 1796, and architect and artist Joseph Gandy was commissioned in 1830 to create a painting of the Bank of England – lying in ruins in the future – to be included on the walls of its own rotunda (Dillon 17). Ruins can thus function as "routes out of our own moment" (53), meaning that they indicate both past states of solidity and future states of decrepitude.

However, sham ruins are not just routes; they have an effect. They can act as a reversal, turning real ruins into fake ones, or vice versa. This is different from real ruins which, as Reza Negarestani indicates in "Undercover Softness: An Introduction to the Architecture and Politics of Decay," foreground the continuum of decay inherent in every object, rather than inserting decay where it does not belong. Negarestani says, "the troubling aspect of decay has to do more with its dynamism or gradation than with its inherently defiling nature" (382). This notion could be extended to all architecture, as David Farrell Krell does, when he says that "The truth of architecture is (in) ruins," meaning that "Architecture is spirit's knee-jerk reaction to nature, and nature inevitably invades even its most sustained constructions" (58). Sham ruins are different. They are not about gradation and decay, at least not at first. They are figures of artifice, intention, and difference.

In other words, rather than fitting in (like in Rome), sham ruins ruin. It was said previously that the oldest sham ruins ruin time because they become indistinguishable from the legitimate past. Once sham ruins enter history, they add a fake history to the real one. Paolo Virno has discussed the way that there are always two pasts, both an old actuality and a potential actuality, different-than-it-was (13). The old actuality is what really was, while the fake past represents potentiality, or difference. Thus, the potential for change only "appears in retrospect" (116), meaning that change is, paradoxically, always "something that was" (117; cf. Chapter 2 of this book), rather than something that will be.

Ruination

However, sham ruins can actually ruin much more than this. Their power to ruin is of a much broader nature. One way to address this topic is through a strategy of interpretation that philosopher Graham Harman calls "ruin-ation" (Harman 38–41). Harman is one of the originators of the burgeoning philosophical movement called speculative realism. These philosophers are basically interested in discussing how objects in the world are impossible for humans ever to know, while at the same time, in a seemingly paradoxical move, they can become known, although this knowledge can only take place indirectly.

While speculative realism applies to every kind of object everywhere, sham ruins are particularly apt for bringing some of the key features of this branch of philosophy to light. Speculative realism posits that there is always something unknown, or withdrawn, about objects. Something always resists not only human knowledge but also the experience of any other object (Willems 127–8). For example, take a stone used to make a sham ruin. A piece of sandstone was excavated from the Grahams Quarry, near Cartworth Fold, just south of Leeds. This stone has been cut, shaped, and dried. It has been ordered, paid for, and transported. An architect has designed the form the stone is to be a part of. The prevailing trends of the time designate that this form should be a sham ruin in a rich person's garden. Workers execute the design, deciding that the stone will function as a quoin, or cornerstone, of the fifth row from the bottom on the south-facing side. This stone is wedged between others, exerting its weight on the stone below it, taking the pressure applied by the stone above. Over the years, the stone dissolves faster and faster. This is because of the growing acidity – or increased hydrogen ions – of the rain, due to pollution. The stone is mocked, along with the sham ruin as a whole, as an architectural embarrassment. Yet all these ways of using and seeing the stone do not exhaust the possibilities of the stone. It could still be used, seen, or experienced in different ways, by both human and other objects, processes, and ideas. In fact, all that any experience of the stone can do is to miss the total experience of the stone. It can only 'ruin' the total experience of the stone.

Yet in this ruined experience of the stone, something is learned about what is ruined. In other words, all these different ways of experiencing the stone still miss something about the stone, something is understood about what is still missing, even if that thing cannot even be guessed at. In this sense, one of Harman's answers to how objects in the world are experienced is that they are experienced through 'ruination.' Meaning is missed in many different ways, yet it is in the plurality of misses that the essence of an object can be known, at least indirectly (Harman 41).

In another example, a joke can be ruined by explaining it literally. So a direct literal explanation 'ruins' a joke. Yet at the same time, what is ruined by literal explanation can be taken as the 'truth' of a joke. Thus, if we ruin something in a bunch of different ways it can create a bunch of different statements about the truth of that object (38). Although it seems like we are a long way from home, it actually answers the question of what do sham ruins ruin, in yet another way: the answer is that they ruin truth.

Another way to approach this is that sham ruins are also called *follies*. Both 'sham' and 'folly' indicate that these ruins are far removed from the truth. They are not what they pretend to be. The winds of time have not blown these stones down. Human hands have arranged them artfully.

Arcadia

The connection between truth and sham ruins is made in one of the most well-known contemporary representations of a sham ruin, Tom Stoppard's play *Arcadia* (1993). The story is located in a country house in Derbyshire, England. Within the garden of the house lies "an eruption of gloomy forest and towering crag, of ruins where there was never a house, of water dashing against rocks where there was neither spring" (Stoppard 15); in other words, a sham ruin. The play alternates between two time periods. Thomasina Coverly is studying mathematics with her tutor Septimus Hodge in the early nineteenth century, and in the late twentieth century, Hannah Jarvis and Bernard Nightingale are each doing their own research into the history of the estate. Throughout the play, the two time periods are intertwined, which is most clearly symbolized by the props from each period remaining on a table, so that laptops and quills sit together in both the past and the present. One prop, a live turtle, plays a part in both periods. The play mainly deals with ideas of chaos theory (Vees-Gulani) and the industrial revolution. However, here the play is used to develop the theory of how sham ruins can be used as a strategy for change.

One of the main themes of the early nineteenth-century part of the story is debunking the notion of a mechanical universe. Thomasina, echoing the thought of astronomer and mathematician Pierre-Simon Laplace (Fleming 56–7), describes this view when she says:

> If you could stop every atom in its position and direction, and if your mind could comprehend all the actions thus suspended, then if you were really, really good at algebra you could write the formula for all the future; and although nobody can be so clever as to do it, the formula must exist just as if one could.
>
> (Stoppard 9–10)

In place of this mechanical model of the universe, the student and teacher develop one of deterministic chaos and entropy, namely, the second law of thermodynamics, which states that the changes a system experiences over time tend toward a state of entropy, and are irreversible. Thomasina asks Septimus about how jam gets mixed in rice pudding when stirred but does not get unmixed when the stirring is reversed. The tutor answers:

> No more you can, time must needs run backward, and since it will not, we must stir our way onward mixing as we go, disorder out of disorder into disorder until pink is complete, unchanging and unchangeable, and we are done with it for ever. This is known as free will or self-determination. (He picks up the tortoise and moves it a few inches as though it had strayed, on top of some loose papers, and admonishes it.)
>
> (9)

However, Thomasina sees the world as more complex, time as nonlinear. The structure of the play also illustrates this point. The props on the table are not taken away, and in the final scene the characters of both periods also appear together, dressed in a similar fashion. This shows that, as Stoppard has said of the play, "in a very crude way the structure of *Arcadia* mimics the reiteration towards chaos, finally" (Kelly and Demastes 5).

On the one hand, the concept of entropy which informs much of Stoppard's play has had a great influence on art theory, including Robert Smithson's "Entropy and the New Monuments" (Smithson), Rudolf Arnheim's "anabolic tendency" (Arnheim 31–2), and Dan Flavin's "inactive history" (Sylvester 167; cf. Chapter 3 of this book). What all these theories share with entropy is that they start with organization and tend toward chaos. Sham ruins are different. They begin in chaos and remain in chaos. Or, as Macaulay argues, they begin in chaos and create more chaos when force people to question the authenticity of the real ruins that follow them.

In *Arcadia*, sham ruins do not challenge the role of entropy in the play, but they should. The character associated with sham ruins is Septimus, the tutor, who is actually a fake hermit hired to accessorize the sham ruin in the country house garden: "The hermit was *placed* in the landscape exactly as one might place a pottery gnome. And there he lived out his life as a garden ornament" (Stoppard 31, emphasis in original). This was not an uncommon occurrence for actual eighteenth-century sham ruins (Dillon 6). The main characteristic of Stoppard's sham hermit is that he takes everything too literally and does not understand Thomasina's advanced theories. Thus, the sham ruin cannot be connected to the most forward-thinking elements in the play. However, in his preliminary notes, Stoppard states, in all caps, that one of the main themes of *Arcadia* is "THE

RECONCILIATION OF DETERMINISM AND THE RANDOM" (Stoppard). If this is really his goal, the sham ruin in his play could have had a much more important role.

Let's go back to the work of Harman in order to better understand how sham ruins can be used to better appreciate the kind of reconciliation Stoppard is aiming for. The theory of a mechanical universe can be simply defined as the theory that current acts are determined by previous acts (or laws of nature). On the other hand, randomness captures the idea that current acts are divorced from previous causes or laws. Following these two choices, the human subject is either inescapably lodged within the mechanics of our world or able, as a self-reflexive creature, to rise above the world and thus be free. Sham ruins are useful for thinking about the way all objects, and not just human ones, mediate between these two options.

In one way, sham ruins are in the world; they are materially contingent. This is perhaps most clearly seen in their political aspects. Since most actual ruins in England are Gothic, and during the Gothic period England was officially Catholic, in the Puritan age sham ruins were seen as a sign of the fragility of Catholicism. However, sham ruins also withdraw from meaning, remaining forever exotic in the words of Kaplan, or they get mixed in with real ruins, as Macaulay describes. The strength of sham ruins, in contradistinction to real ones, lies in their mediation between both poles. This mediation means that, like the humorous core of a joke, sham ruins are withdrawn from complete knowledge, but not totally removed from human understanding. Or, as Harman says:

> we are *unfree* rather than free; being just what we are, we are incapable of anything else. Yet in a sense we are always *inside* the world through the fact that we are made of pieces – and only *therefore* are we free, with our components doing the work of liberty on our behalf. For there is an excess in our pieces beyond what is needed to create us, and this excess allows new and unexpected things to happen.
>
> (Harman 75)

Sham ruins can surprise us because the knowledge they represent is broken, and thus new knowledge is possible. And what seems shocking now is that some people at the time of Sanderson's folly did not seem to mind. As Clark says:

> the frame of mind which could find delight in canvas pinnacles is strangely different from our own. . . . We are incapable of isolating the sensation and of enjoying a dramatic effect without the interference of truth, and there has come to be something shocking in the discovery

that a seeming castle is only a distinguished cowshed. It is a sham; it is telling a lie.

(56–7)

Knowledge has always broken knowledge. Sham ruins are just visible representations of this truth. Ian Bogost makes a similar point in his discussion of the film *Men in Black* (1997) when he says that:

> Partitioned like so many galaxies, each thing, from leavener bubble to pound cake, from mathematical operand to robotic companion, from opium poppy to criminal justice system, each demands its own broken knowledge. Weird, tiny, totalities simultaneously run their own rules and participate in the dominion of others around them. Each things remains alien to every other, operationally as well as physically. To wonder is to respect things as things in themselves.
>
> (130–1)

The sense of wonder that Bogost describes is a response to the withdrawn nature of objects. But at the same time the multiple interpretations of what sham ruins mean indicate that they lie in a multitude of ways. This is the key to the way they work. What is important about sham ruins is not what they ruin, but rather that they ruin, that they are able to ruin. This is also the key for uncovering the sham ruins of our own age.

New Sham Ruins

For example, on June 11, 1986, the Pittsburgh Post-Gazette published an article called "Fashion Trend Full of Holes" by Peter Leo. It was on an up-and-coming fad, buying a new pair of jeans with pre-ripped holes. In the article, Leo is surprised to find a new product that is sold already-ruined: "The holes will be put in at the factory" (4) he says. Citing the preplanned obsolesce of cars and the holes in Swiss cheese as tongue-in-cheek predecessors, the writer then posits starting his own line of Leo-brand sham ruins, "including the pre-scratched stereo record, preworn docksiders and the pre-eaten house plant, already ravaged by bugs" (ibid.). Although Leo focuses on explaining the style as a marketing gimmick, he also provides an early indication of an interest in objects bought already broken.

The first iPhone came out on June 29, 2007. On a website dated exactly 1 month later, professional magician and science fiction writer Andrew Mayne already listed numerous apps to make it look ruined: Damaged Beyond All Repaired (*sic*), Missing Icons, Frozen Screen, Hole in Screen, and the simply titled Broken (Mayne). These apps are listed as 'Screen Pranks,' and the aim seems to be to load them on the phones of other people in order to make them think their apparatus has gone kaput. Not many would be fooled by such a trick today. Yet cracked screen apps are still popular. This is one of the things that make such apps contemporary sham ruins: pleasure in a broken object does not diminish when this brokenness is fake and purchased online.

For the South Korean Gwangju Design Biennale of 2011, a number of architects[2] designed new *Urban Follies* on sites in the southern city's old center which was destroyed during the Japanese occupation in the first half of the twentieth century (Lee and Lee 160). Thus, these Urban Follies, even before their forms were known, were already loaded cultural objects, referencing not only the occupation but also, among other events, the Gwangju People's Uprising of 1980, which took place after the assassination of Park Chung-hee (who had been in power since 1961) and the rule of Park's successor, Chun Doohwan, who was no less dictatorial. In Gwangju, students and workers who had been the fodder for the rapid industrialization of the country formed unions and protested, leading to:

> an explosion of the confrontation, in its most antagonistic form, between the ruling classes and the ruled classes, mingled with other complicated elements in a certain time and place, which was formed by hierarchical and national contradictions, and developed into a confrontation between democracy and dictatorship at a certain point in history.
>
> (Kim Se-gyun qtd. in Ahn 28)

That this group of architects would devise projects in the form of follies (as mentioned previously, a close cousin to the sham ruin) is indicative of the manner in which purposely broken objects can function.

For this project, architect Florian Beigel created a work called "Seowonmoon Lantern" which was located at the former Seowon Gate and is an oversized version of a traditional Korean lantern, which was also constructed around and over the May 18 Democratic Uprising Monument. As stated in the biennale catalog, "The locus of our attention" with the Urban Follies is the "disjunction between form and performance" (Gwangju Biennale 11). The form of Beigel's work is the traditional lantern, but the performance of it, making it larger and thus turning it into a small theater, bus stop, or other space, making it: "not difficult to see that this urban artefact substituted the value of civil spirit towards justice and democracy against military dictatorship and maybe perhaps something that needs to be kept in mind in the steps towards the future, with an image of a traditional lantern in Korea" (Lee and Lee 160), thus acting as a kind of "intrusive novelty" (ibid.).

Within the reception and historicization of the Uprising in a country which elected Park's daughter Park Geun-hye as president from 2013 to 2017, when she was impeached because of corruption.

In another example, the Android smartwatch Samsung Galaxy Gear was first released in September 2013. A year later, Corbin Davenport uploaded a video to YouTube showing how to hack the phone and install Windows 95 on it (Davenport). Davenport's hack did not turn the watch into a piece of nostalgia as much as it was a comment on the negative reception the device got because of its own lack of functionality. In this sense, the hack merely foregrounded the way that the unhacked watch was already, although unintentionally, a sham ruin.

The meaning of each of these diverse, new sham ruins depends on the context of its construction; ripped jeans do not mean the same thing as a recontextualized memorial in Gwangju. Yet using sham ruins as both an architectural feature and a concept can group otherwise completely disparate contemporary objects together. Similarities are found which are not so apparent when seeing each object in its own context.

First, the fascination with sham objects seems to be more widespread than ever. In fact, new objects are being turned into sham ruins almost as soon as they are released. This is a sign that we are back in a Victorian frame of mind which, as Clark indicates, has no problem with finding pleasure in a lie. This view of sham ruins can be found not only in 'authentic' Pioneer and Civil War villages found throughout the United States but also in the fantastic constructions of Disneyland and the Epcot center. In "The Necessity for Ruins," J.B. Jackson argues that these constructions are referring to a different past than traditional monuments, "a vernacular past, a golden age where there are no dates or names, simply a sense of the way it *used to be*, history as the chronicle of everyday existence" (94–5). This is different from the empty exoticism of Kaplan. Instead, it is a representation of a past without a definite beginning date to celebrate, a past that is "legendary, half-forgotten" (100), rather than simply unknown.

On the other hand, it is not just that more objects are being turned into sham ruins, but, as Himali Singh Soin shows throughout her blog *The Paris Follies*, the sham ruin quality of all objects is becoming more apparent. By looking at such objects as Benard Tschumi's follies in Paris' Parc de la Villette or empty picture frames in a Rue de Turenne courtyard Soin shows how sham ruins can be found in a variety of situations (Soin). This is one of the reasons that Harman's work is so important for this discussion: it focuses on the mediation between an object's known and unknown properties. Following the thought of Evan Calder Williams, all objects are "hostile," meaning that "The assumed correlation between the intended purpose of objects and their actual behavior is shattered" (20, cf. Chapter 4 of this book). Sham ruins mirror what Williams calls a "particular hostility" because they sabotage the idea of purpose in the way "There is something particular about this thing that acts in a manner that cannot be understood in terms of its intended functions" (27).

We are creating objects which do not function as they should all the time. And perhaps we should let them work for us rather than clutter our inboxes and junk drawers with unwanted debris. This is Hito Steyerl's argument in "The Spam of the Earth," in which she says:

> Dense clusters of radio waves leave our planet every second. Our letters and snapshots, intimate and official communications, TV broadcasts and text messages drift away from earth in rings, a tectonic architecture of the desires and fears of our times. In a few hundred thousand years, extraterrestrial forms of intelligence may incredulously sift through our wireless communications. But imagine the perplexity of those creatures when they actually look at the material. Because a huge percentage of the pictures inadvertently sent off into deep space is actually spam. Any archaeologist, forensic, or historian – in this world or another – will look at it as our legacy and our likeness, a true portrait of our times and ourselves. Imagine a human reconstruction somehow made from this digital rubble. Chances are, it would look like image spam.
>
> (161)

Spam is a sham ruin because it purposefully does not work, and the work it does not do is representation. Spam excludes the individual in favor of the hegemonic, in order to appeal to the widest target audience possible. Thus, Steyerl asks, "What if image spam thus became a record of a widespread refusal, a withdrawal of people from representation?" (165). The images going out into space are a mixture of spam and images of our most intimate moments, stolen by exes, posted on revenge porn sites, and thus preserved for infinity for alien archeologists to discover. Yet by being mixed in with spam, spam acts as their protector. The banality of spam mixes in with the personal nature of the other images. And like one of the functions of sham ruins mentioned previously, spam images can ruin the authenticity of these other images. The purposely fake nature of spam puts the authentic nature of personal images in question, thus protecting our past from the excavations of the future (173). Thus, it should not be taken that the sham ruins of the present are the same as those of the past. Contemporary sham ruins can be carried around in a pocket. They can shift between being functional and nonfunctional by simply opening and closing an app. They are going out into space. And sometimes they are not originally intended to be sham ruins but are turned into them by user intervention.

And once these different objects are all gathered together under the common term of 'sham ruins,' the truth that they all ruin becomes apparent. One thing that contemporary sham ruins seem to be doing is attacking user-friendliness. Although there are huge open source and DYI communities out there, most of the objects we use are closed off behind single buttons and warranty-invalidating contract agreements. Breaking these objects is a way of making them do things they are not meant to do, even if that new thing is simply not to work. Contemporary sham ruins are therefore political not in the sense of critiquing a specific ideology but by claiming new uses for old objects. The way this is done is by breaking them in different ways.

In Leo's 1986 article on pre-ripped jeans, he complains that "Hey you don't get something for nothing, assuming you consider a hole something" (4). Contemporary sham objects show that a hole is something. A hole can be a strategy for using objects in new and inventive ways.

Notes

1. An article by The Folly Fellowship argues that early sham ruins seemed to have "failed to capture the imagination of the Duke [of Urbino's] friends and contemporaries' and were thus limited to less permanent structures such as stage sets or the ruin rooms of the Palazzo de Te in Rome" (Folly Fellowship 1), although another example could be found in the same Palazzo's *spezzato* style of plastering, in which new plaster is made to look broken.
2. Florian Beigel; Peter Eisenman; Juan Herreros; Sungryong Joh; S.H. Jung and S.J. Kim; Dominique Perrault; Francisco Sanin; Nader Tehrani; Yoshiharu Tsukamoto; and Alejandro Zaera-Polo.

Works Cited

Ahn, Jean. "The Socio-Economic Background of the Gwangju Uprising." In *South Korean Democracy: Legacy of the Gwangju Uprising*. Eds. Georgy Katsiaficas and Na Kahn-chae. London: Routledge, 2018: 24–46.

Arnheim, Rudolf. *Entropy and Art: An Essay on Disorder and Order*. Berkeley: University of California Press, 1971.

Bogost, Ian. *Alien Phenomenology: Or What It's Like to Be a Thing*. Minneapolis; London: University of Minnesota Press, 2012.

Bourriaud, Nicolas. *The Exform*. Trans. Erik Butler. London; New York: Verso, 2016.

Bratton, Denise. "Rome, Broken City." *Cabinet*, Vol. 20 (Winter 2005/2006): 100–1.

Breisach, Ernst. *Historiography: Ancient, Medieval, and Modern*. Chicago: Chicago University Press, 2007.

Clark, Kenneth. *The Gothic Revival: An Essay in the History of Taste.* New York: Harper & Row, 1972.

Davenport, Corbin. "*Doom* on Android Wear." *YouTube* (Oct 1, 2014). Internet: www.youtube.com/watch?v=1ei2-jBGGYk.

Dillon, Brian. "Fragments from a History of Ruin." *Cabinet*, Vol. 20 (Winter 2005/2006): 55–9.

Dillon, Brian. *Ruin Lust: Artists' Fascination with Ruins, from Turner to the Present Day.* London: Tate Publishing, 2014.

Fleming, John. *Tom Stoppard's Arcadia.* London; New York: Bloomsbury, 2008.

Folly Fellowship, The. "Sham Ruins." *Foll-e*, Vol. 45 (Aug 2012): 1–4.

Gilpin, William. *Observations, Relative Chiefly to Picturesque Beauty, Made in the Year 1772, on Several Parts of England: Particularly the Mountains, and Lakes of Cumberland, and Westmoreland.* Vol 1. London: Printed for R. Blamire, Strand, 1776.

Gwangju, Biennale. *Gwangju Design Biennale 2011* (2011). Internet: http://gb.or.kr/?mid=sub_eng&mode=03&sub=01&tab=2011_01.

Harman, Graham. *Circus Philosophicus.* Hants: Zero Books, 2010.

Harman, Graham. *Weird Realism: Lovecraft and Philosophy.* Hants: Zero Books, 2012.

Headley, Gwyn and Wim Meulenkamp. *The English Folly: The Edifice Complex.* Liverpool: Liverpool University Press, 2020.

Howley, James. *The Follies and Garden Buildings of Ireland.* New Haven: Yale University Press, 2004.

Jackson, J.B. "The Necessity for Ruins." In *The Necessity for Ruins and Other Topics.* Amherst: The University of Massachusetts Press, 1980: 89–102.

Kaplan, Lauren. "Exotic Follies: Sanderson Miller's Mock Ruins." *Frame*, Vol. 1 (Spring 2011): 54–68.

Kelly, Katerine and William Demastes. "The Playwright and the Professors: An Interview with Tom Stoppard." *South Central Review*, Vol. 11, No. 4 (Winter 1994): 1–14.

Krell, David Farrell. *Architicture: Ecstasies of Space, Time, and the Human Body.* Albany: State University of New York Press, 1997.

Lee, Min Jung and Dong-Eon Lee. "An Interpretation of the Urban Folly in Gwangju, South Korea through the Lens of Contextual Novelty." *Architectural Research*, Vol. 18, No. 4 (2016): 157–64.

Leo, Peter. "Fashion Trend Full of Holes." *Pittsburgh Post-Gazzette, City/Area* (Jun 11, 1986): 4.

Macaulay, Rose. *Pleasure of Ruins.* New York: Walker and Col., 1966.

Mayne, Andrew. "Tricks and Pranks for the iPhone." *itricks.com* (Jul 2007). Internet: http://itricks.com/iphone/.

McAleer, J. Philip. "St. Mary's (1820–1830), Halifax: An Early Example of the Use of Gothic Revival Forms in Canada." *Journal of the Society of Architectural Historians*, Vol. 45, No. 2 (Jun 1986): 134–47.

Mumford, Lewis. *Sticks and Stones: A Study of American Architecture and Civilization.* New York: Dover, 1955.

Negarestani, Reza. "Undercover Softness: An Introduction to the Architecture and Politics of Decay." *Collapse*, Vol. 6 (2010): 379–430.

Perusse, Lyle. "The Gothic Revival in California, 1850–1890." *Journal of the Society of Architectural Historians*, Vol. 14, No. 3 (Oct 1955): 15–22.

Robinson, William. *The Parks and Gardens of Paris: Considered in Relation to the Wants of Other Cities and of the Public and Private Gardens: Being Notes on a Study of Paris*. Paris: J. Murray, 1883.

Ruskin, John. *The Stones of Venice, Vol. 1: The Foundations*. London: Smith, Elder and Co., 1858.

Smithson, Robert. "Entropy and the New Monuments." In *Robert Smithson: The Collected Writings*. Ed. Jack Flam. Berkeley: University of California Press, 1996: 10–23.

Soin, Himali Singh. "The Paris Follies." *ArtSlant* (Mar 31, 2015). Internet: www.artslant.com/ber/articles/show/42519-the-paris-follies.

Stewart, David. "Political Ruins: Gothic Sham Ruins and the '45." *Journal of the Society of Architectural Historians*, Vol. 55, No. 4 (Dec 1996): 400–11.

Steyerl, Hito. "The Spam of the Earth: Withdrawal from Representation." In *The Wretched of the Screen*. Berlin: Sternberg Press, 2012: 160–75.

Stoppard, Tom. *Arcadia*. New York: Farrar, Straus and Giroux, 1994.

Stoppard, Tom. *Arcadia, by Sir Tom Stoppard: Notes and Early Sectional Drafts*. Add MS 89037/1/1: 1991.

Sylvester, David. *Interviews with American Artists*. New Haven: Yale University Press, 2001.

Vasari, Giorgio. *Lives of the Painters, Sculptures and Architects*. Trans. Graston du C. de Vere. 4 Vols. New York: Everyman's Library, 1996.

Vees-Gulani, Susanne. "Hidden Order in the 'Stoppard Set': Chaos Theory in the Content and Structure of Tom Stoppard's *Arcadia*." *Theatre and Performance Studies*, Vol. 42, No. 3 (Fall 1999): 411–26.

Viney, William. *Waste: A Philosophy of Things*. London; New York: Bloomsbury, 2014.

Virno, Paolo. *Déjà Vu and the End of History*. Trans. David Broder. London: Verso, 2015.

Willems, Brian. *Shooting the Moon*. Hants: Zero Books, 2015.

Williams, Evan Calder. "Hostile Object Theory." In *Spooky Action: A Materialist Nightmare*. Ed. Patricia Margarita Hernandez. Miami: [NAME] Publications, 2016: 18–40.

Wölfflin, Heinrich. *Principles of Art History: The Problem of the Development of Style in Later Art*. New York: Dover, 1950.

2   The Potential of the Past

The sub-genre of alternate history is often maligned in science fiction studies. Alternate histories are considered to be rife with militarism (Rickels 91–3) or to be so dystopian that they just make readers thankful they live in the age they do (Duncan 216); in addition, they are accused of having little to do with science, merely being an excuse for Puck-like rollicking adventures to take place (Booker and Thomas 23) along the lines of *Bill and Ted's Excellent Adventure* (1989). When alternate histories do find themselves praised it is because they are seen as holding a mirror to the contemporary situation, as Maurice Blanchot claims is the "proper" use of science fiction in general (Blanchot). Alternative histories which fit this bill show how writing history is really about writing the present (Hellekson 35–6); this means that such works are taken as serious explanations of current social and spatial issues (Warf 18).

However, Aleksei Fedorchenko's *Pervye na Lune/First on the Moon* (2005) suggests that alternative histories can have another agenda. And the film does so in the form of a sham ruin. So far, sham ruins have taken the shape of not just architecture but also torn jeans and phone apps. Starting with this chapter, the idea of sham ruins developed previously is abstracted into a general concept, meaning a reading of *purposely wasteful* objects of *artifice, intention, and difference* which have an *unexpected function*. Fodorchenko's film fits into all of these aspects of sham ruins and focuses on another: *reaching out into the past, unsettling knowledge about the ruins that came before, and of those out into the future, invalidating the real ruins to come.*

Purporting to be a documentary showing that Russia actually landed on the moon in the 1930s, the film places the cosmonauts on the lunar surface long before the Americans. Yet the film is less a skewed reflection of current woes than *a mediation on the relationship between the past and possibility*. In other words, if alternative histories are derided for eschewing the more traditional view of science fiction which sees change located in the

DOI: 10.4324/9781003213086-2

future (Booker and Thomas 23; Scholes 17–18), *First on the Moon* suggests that the future is on lock-down, meaning that the limitless possibilities of what-is-to-come have already been decided for us (Shaviro 32; Srnicek and Williams). Paradoxically, the films suggest that it is *the past* which needs to be looked to in order to begin imagining alternatives to the present. This is where the film most clearly intersects with the sham ruin, in that they both invalidate the past in order to create something new. In fact, this idea is taken to the extreme: *First on the Moon* shows that *potentiality is only located in the past and never in the future*. It is in this sense that alternative histories can be considered 'true' science fiction along the most conservative grounds in that they provide representations of an unexpected future; the only difference is that these representations are located in the past.

Obviously Fake

First on the Moon pretends to be a League of Nations-commissioned documentary aimed at telling the story of how the Soviet Union was actually the first country to put a human on the moon in 1938, Ivan Kharlamov (Boris Vlasov). The film opens with an archeological dig which has uncovered the remains of Kharlamov's return capsule. It is then seen that Kharlamov survived, although he escaped the attention of the authorities by assuming different identities on Earth and doing his best to remain in hiding. The bulk of the film shows the training and selection program for the cosmonauts for Kharlamov's mission.

The initial sequence of the film begins with an apology for the quality of the archival material from the 1930s, thus making a commonplace connection in alternative history films between authenticity of material and lack in the quality of the material presented (Anderson 72–3). However, the film immediately diverges from the tradition of alternative history because the first set of images presented indicates the *false* nature of the footage rather than its validity. The initial shot in the film first seems to be of the lunar surface since it features a barren, rocky surface. The main titles of the film are imposed over this image, thus giving it some weight. Then a hoe is used to begin digging into the hard ground.

At first it seems that this is the scene of a lunar excavation site, but it is soon revealed that it is actually people in northern Chile digging up what they believe are the remains of a crashed meteorite (which turns out to be the debris of Kharlamov's landing module). In other words, the person using the hoe is seen to be a local of the region rather than a cosmonaut. Thus, the film opens with an image that is first taken to be of the moon but is then shown to be false. This should be taken as reading strategy for all of the lunar images in the film, as well as sham ruins in general.

Thus, the opening of the film is obviously fake. Daria Kabanova has described this sequence as follows: "What is being shown is not what it seems, but rather what the camera made it look like. The opening shot draws attention to the film's own cinematic apparatus from the very beginning" (79). According to this argument, there should be no tension between the real and the fake, for it is shown at the beginning that the film is just a trick. Yet the opening sequence is soon forgotten by Kabanova, who goes on to read the film the traditional vein of the mockumentary by foregrounding a tension between found footage and newly shot material:

> The film holds the viewer within this interpretative uncertainty for its whole duration. In a way, this allows the film to keep the interpretative field open, without the necessity to assign one single reading to Soviet history, and to make this history into a source of now post-Soviet cultural myths about the origins of contemporary Russian culture. The blurry boundary between fact and fiction, between art and life, on which Soviet textuality was predicated, made it especially conducive for creating cultural mythologies.
>
> (90)

This imagined tension between real and found footage has been at the heart of most readings of the film. In fact, in the year of its release the film won the Venice Horizons Documentary Award at the Venice Film Festival, a prize otherwise given to documentary films. It is unclear whether the festival organizers were aware of the nature of the film (Prokhorov), which actually contains only 7% of actual archival footage (Rogatchevski 256). This is even more surprising since the opening sequence is not the only indication of the clearly fake nature of the film. Other indications can be seen, for example, in the manner in which the potential cosmonauts are filmed during their training. There needs to be a reason in the film logic for the existence of intimate recordings of the cosmonauts in their quarters and so on, so it is posited that they are under constant filmic surveillance and that this footage has survived. However, not only is this footage of a much higher quality than that of actual found footage which is used but also there are camera angles which, although theoretically accountable, seem to belie the documentary nature of the film, as seen in an over-the-shoulder shot of cosmonaut candidate Nadezhda Svetlaya (Viktoriya Ilyinskaya) looking into a mirror, which would be particularly difficult to obtain via surveillance cameras.

Thus *First on the Moon* is not about the tension between documentary and mockumentary footage, but is rather, as Darren Jorgensen argues, about recovering "the history of Soviet space travel in order to aestheticise it"

(210), meaning that "The most disturbing elements of the Soviet space program, such as cruel training schemes and pathological secrecy, turn here into an aesthetic that betrays something of a fondness for the old regime" (212). Yet if this is true, why the confusion in Venice, and the backtracking of Kabanova? On the one hand, it is because, despite shots such as the one of Svetlaya in the mirror, great care was taken by cinematographer Anatoli Lesnikov in recreating documentary-style footage of the time. For, as Oleg Kovalov states:

> Every shot in the film seems to have been taken with a camera of the period represented on the screen; so it appears that the film has been shot with dozens of cameras. Every piece of 'film-footage' comes with a made-up 'history'; the skillful imitation of defects in the footage (or, on the contrary, their absence) suggest how each was shot and where it was stored. Fedorchenko lovingly reproduces the intertitles found in film-journals and even the fonts used in old subtitles. . . . While there is a mass of external gradations in the texture of the images, the 'super-quality' of Fedorchenko's shots lies in the fact that they graphically convey the gradations of historical time.
>
> (Kovalov)

Yet all of this attention to detail functions more to call attention to the constructedness of the film rather than to function as a vehicle for Kobanova's "interpretative uncertainty" (90). The position of the film is clear: it is a sham. It is not, as Julia Vassilieva argues, that:

> The power of the film's statement comes from its skillful adoption of the postmodern paradigm, since effectively it is saying that, in this fully constructed world, we are free to choose a version of the past and the present to live by.
>
> (Vassilieva)

To reinforce the point, traces of the fake are found elsewhere throughout the film. During a scene where Svetlaya and Kharlamov are in a classroom explaining to a young boy about the 'seriousness' of their training, three different lunar representations are shown in a single shot. On the wall is a map of either deep craters or volcanic activity on the moon. An image stuck on the blackboard is a photograph taken through a telescope. But the most interesting lunar representation in this shot is the lunar globe, with the far side of the moon covered in a deep black, as if nothing could penetrate its unknowability (the first images of the far side of the moon were taken in the 1950s by the Soviet Luna flyby missions).

And yet this globe quickly reflects a similar state of constructedness as argued for the earlier scenes previously. The following scene is just too 'set up' to be natural. First, Kharlamov introduces another cosmonaut, Duska, who is a monkey. Then there are some edits which defy continuity. Kharlamov is seen comparing himself to Duska who is strapped into the position the monkey will occupy during the flight. The monkey is confined inside a metal mold, arms outstretched, as if being crucified. Kharlamov, facing Duska, stretches his arms out in a similar position as a voice-over says that Duska has a 1% chance of survival. Cleary both are being sacrificed for the sake of the moon journey.

The nonrealistic nature of this scene is then supported by a shot with Kharlamov on his own with the moon globe. The background is darkened, and he slowly caresses the surface. While at first this gesture simply indicates his thinking about the moon, it also indicates the physicality of the construction of the moon under his fingertips. This physicality was shown in an earlier scene when Duska was seen jumping on the globe, and it is continued in this shot when Kharlamov sets his hat on it a few moments later.

This scene is not only about the dangers of the lunar mission but also about one of the causes of such dangers: the construction of the knowledge of the moon is partial, and may be wrong, which could lead to disastrous results. The number of simultaneous representations of the moon in this scene, the deep black of the unknown lunar far side, and the emphasis of the physical construction of the moon globe all stress the image of the moon which is constructed.

These lunar images can be called *haptic* not because touch is literally involved but because the issue of the physicality of an object brings the larger elements of the film's structure as a whole into focus. As Laura Marks argues in *Touch* one of the most important elements of haptic visuality is that the viewer concentrates on the "surface," or "skin" of the image:

> Haptic looking tends to reset on the surface of its object rather than to plunge into depth, not to distinguish form so much as to discern texture. It is a labile, plastic sort of look, more inclined to move than to focus. The video works I propose to call haptic invite a look that moves on the surface plane of the screen for some time before the viewer realises what it is she is beholding. Haptic video resolves into figuration only gradually if at all, instead inviting the caressing look I have described.
> (8)

It is not that this scene dissolves and resolves into figuration as Marks calls for. Everything is very clearly shot. However, when Kharlamov is left alone with the globe the film indicates that it is entering a theatrical dimension by blackening out the background. Theatricality is also why continuity is less important in this scene. Kharlamov is simply shown running his hand along the surface of the globe, skipping across its craters. This draws the viewer's attention to the realm of touch, into thinking about what the moon, or at least what a globe of the moon, feels like. Then when the cosmonaut rests his hat on the globe it is clear that "the surface of the object" is being called into play. The consequence of this scene is the same as the first images of the fake lunar surface which turned into a Chilean archeology site: it is not the moon which is being shown, but constructions of it. In other words, at this point in this film there is no tension between archival and actual footage: the moon, and the journey to it, is all fake. This point is made with such obviousness in *First on the Moon* in order for the end of the film to have the power that it does, since it breaks with the obviously fake images seen thus far by presenting two shockingly 'real' images of the actual Soviet lunar journey and landing.

The Past Is the Future

Yet before a discussion of the end of the film can take place, the connection between the constructedness of the film and its figuration of an alternative past needs to be developed. This is especially important in the context of sham ruins since, in the words of Rory Fraser, "these small, often forgotten buildings offer us an alternative view into the periods in which they were built; a diagonal glimpse of a soft underbelly that is rarely seen" (4). In a similar manner, the film depicts an alternative history of the space race: the Soviets got there first. Yet at the same time the way in which this past is constructed is seen as obviously fake; as Asif Siddiqi puts it:

> Ultimately, the movie is a project of a historical recovery that exists in the margins between what happened and was lost, and what never happened but was re-recreated; that is, a perfect summation of the conflicting forces acting on space nostalgia in the post-Soviet space.
>
> (300)

Yet despite numerous readings of the film to the contrary, there is really no tension between found footage and footage produced especially for the film. In fact, to read the film in this way is to miss one of its most interesting aspects: that the construction of an obviously fake alternate past is the only way that potentiality can ever be represented.

In *Déjà Vu and the End of History*, Paolo Virno makes a similar argument about history, meaning that there is an equivalence to be drawn between the past and potential (61). While it seems that the future should be the location of new and vibrant possibilities for action, Virno makes the paradoxical claim that such potentiality is actually something which comes before, not something which lies ahead.

Virno sees the future closed off by the feeling of déjà vu, which arises out of the process of memory creation. Memory is created out of the present, not out of the past. If I do not create a memory of an event in the present, there is no 'material' to create a memory of it in the future (unless it is a false memory, as in seemingly remembering your first birthday party because you have seen pictures of it). The feeling of déjà vu takes place when this memory-creating process becomes palpable (7), meaning that an awareness of the creation of memories takes place during the creation of memories. In this way, a "*memory of the present*" (46) arises, which makes everything seem inevitable. Thus, a sense of déjà vu makes the present seem to be a memory, which makes the present seem mapped out, like it has already happened before. To take the feeling a step further, if the present is already decided, why would the future be any different?

This has much to do with the feeling of seeing a sham ruin. In addition, similar arguments have been formulated before, including Fredric Jameson's reading of the lack of critical tools for dealing with postmodern spatial categories (11), Marc Augé's argument that "we are no longer capable of addressing our relation to space and time . . . except by means of artefacts elaborated by industry and available on the market" which is due to a number of demographic, aesthetic, cultural, physical, and metaphysical changes in scale (60; 52–7), and what Bernard Stiegler calls "symbolic misery," meaning the manner in which "*aesthetic conditioning* . . . has replaced aesthetic experience, making it *impossible*" (3). While Juliane Rebentisch offers a less pessimistic view in her argument that an "anti-teleological time if aesthetic experience" is starting to become possible through nonmusical-based spatializing tendencies (Rebentisch 209), Virno's reading of the location of potentiality in the past rather than the future finds particular resonance in *First on the Moon* and for sham ruins in general.

For Virno, potential is located in the past because:

> Potential is that which is not *yet* actual (but can become so) whereas the actual is that which is *no longer* potential (but once was). This pair express the articulation of earlier and later, the preceding and the subsequent, the past and present.

(63)

Thus, because potentiality cannot coincide with the present and because the present is actual, it must become "an object of memory" (72).

Yet there is not just one memory but two, and this is where alternative histories come in, and where *First on the Moon* comes in in particular; every present has a *double past*, meaning both an *old actuality* and *potentiality, or not-now* (113). The *old actuality* is what was, but the *not-now* of the past is actually potentiality. In this sense, for potentiality, "its positive character appears *in retrospect*" (116), meaning that potentiality is always *"something that was"* (117). Here lies the importance of the obviously sham nature of *First on the Moon*: if the film were to pretend to be an actual history, as its prize at the Venice festival for best documentary film seems to indicate, then it would be a representation, even if a false one, of the *first past*, meaning of an *old actuality*. Although the film is not a real documentary, it would still follow the structure of being *an old truth*. However, "Fodorchenko remakes these sequences in order to emphasise their ridiculousness" (Jorgensen 214), meaning the film is posited as something that obviously did not happen. Yet at the same time this ridiculousness is located in the past. The combination of these two factors locates the film in Virno's *second past*, meaning that of *what did not happen but could have*, and thus of potentiality. In fact, for Virno this is the *only* location for potentiality, at least for a present that is closed off by the wet blanket of déjà vu.

Being located in the *second past* is what separates *First on the Moon* from a similarly structured film, *Opération Lune* made by William Karel for Arte in 2002. Karel's film is a mockumentary which purports to tell the history of how Stanley Kubrick was hired to prepare the recording of a fake moon landing in case the real one did not work out. Much effort was undertaken to make at least the first half of *Opération Lune* seem as realistic as possible. Buzz Aldrin and Kubrick's widow Christiane Kubrick, among others, had interviews repurposed into supporting Karel's story. Although by the end of the film there are abundant clues which indicate that the game is clearly up, as a whole *Opération Lune* functions as a film which pretends to represent the *first history*, meaning that of *an old actuality*, although this old actuality is fake. Because *First on the Moon*, on the other hand, begins from the position of being obviously fake (rather than ending there), it is able to better represent the past as a location of potentiality. Yet the focal object for both films is the same: the moon. This raises the question of whether there is anything qualitatively different about a lunar location for the potentiality of the past.

The Moon

The moon is a privileged setting for a discussion of the relationship between the past and possibility in terms of sham ruins because it *used to be* an object of wild speculation until landing on it proved that it was, as Carl

Sagan succinctly put it, "a static, airless, waterless, black-sky, dead world" (204). Put otherwise, the only time that the moon was seen as an object of potentiality was in the past, while after 1969 it became an object of little interest; the title of Robert Cooper's article on the 1969 moon landings for the *New Yorker* aptly describes what the moon had become: "A Reporter at Large: Men on the Moon (I – Just One Big Rockpile)" (Cooper).

However, this reading of the moon is a bit too stark; it is not that once we landed on the moon it suddenly lost all interest. Rather, as Thomas Disch has argued, its function simply changed from being an object of science fiction to being an object of fantasy:

> In the time of Lucian of Samasota, or even of Cyrano de Bergerac, a trip to the moon was the stuff of fantasy. Once such a voyage began to seem a concrete possibility, science fiction established itself as a separate genre, but the tropism toward fantasy remained in its genes, and now that the moon and Mars and most of our solar system have come to seem real – but barren – destinations, SF has reverted to its origins as fantasy. For every SF story that posits interstellar travel and adventures among aliens is a trip to Oz, given what we know of interstellar distance and the constraints of relativity theory.
>
> As Robert Heinlein observed, in another context, the moon is a harsh mistress.
>
> (77)

On the one hand, the moon underwent a much earlier transformation, for understanding the gravitational relationship between the moon and the earth was how Isaac Newton was able to locate the wheat in the chaff in the thought of Kepler and Galileo (Koestler 504–9). Yet the lunar change that Disch indicates is different, in that it colors not just the present but the past. Thus, the return to fantasy from early interest in the moon in proto-science fiction (cf. Bailey 16–22) that Disch indicates is something that is not only reflected in contemporary iterations of the moon in films such as *The Adventures of Pluto Nash* (2002) but also injected into the science fictional representations of pre-1969 lunar reality. In *Transformers 3* (2011), NASA picks up signals of a lunar crash in 1961 and then develops the Apollo missions in order to discover what actually landed on the moon (a Transformer spaceship) (Willems 168). In *Iron Sky* (2012), a group of Nazis secretly escape to the moon after the Second World War (170). Both of these films have a similar strategy for making the contemporary moon strange – by injecting fantasy into its recent past – and thus seem to show that Disch's lunar return to fantasy has even penetrated contemporary visions of the pre-fantasy past.

In this way, the possibilities of contemporary moon films and novels to envision the past are closed off by the limitations of the present: the moon is a figure of fantasy now, and this limits the manner in which it is forward- and backward-projected. The prevalence of the fantasy of the present has a similar function to the limiting effects of déjà vu. As stated earlier, in order for memory to be created, it must be created in the present; the feeling of déjà vu is the "untrammeled extension of memory's jurisdiction" (Virno 7) in the present with the consequence that "every act and every word that I say and do now seems destined to repeat, step by step, the course that fixes back then, without the possibility of omitting or changing anything" (8). Here, Virno is basing his thought on Henri Bergson's "Memory of the Present and False Recognition" (Bergson), and another Bergson-commentator, Gilles Deleuze, can be used to bring out the way that such limitations of the present turn into limitations of the future. In *Bergsonism*, Deleuze states that:

> if the real is said to resemble the possible, is this not in fact because the real was expected to come about by its own means, to 'project back-wards' a fictitious image of it, and to claim that it was possible at any time, before it happened? In fact, it is not the real that resembles the possible, but the possible that resembles the real, because it has been abstracted from the real once made, arbitrarily extracted from the real like a sterile double.
>
> (98)

The future is the "sterile double" of the possibilities of the present. Yet with déjà vu, this anastrophic projecting backward is more specifically the consequence of a present that is "only apparent repetition" (Virno 7) of the past. In other words, if the present has already been decided, then the future will seem to project back the same sense of decision and we are going nowhere at all. *First on the Moon* is being posited as a film which offers a strategy for circumventing such a stalemate. What is paradoxical about the film is that it does so by looking to the past, which seems to be the source of all the trouble in the first place.

The moon is an object rife with the past. In a physical sense, the lack of an atmosphere on the moon means that its surface is relatively stable, at least in comparison to that of the earth. This means that there is compara-tively more 'old' surface of the moon still visible than on the earth; as Bernd Brunner puts it:

> More than three-quarters of the surface of the Earth is less than two hundred million years old, and virtually nothing on Earth's surface

is the same as it was at the time of its formation. In contrast, according to the most recent estimates, 99 percent of the surface of the moon is more than three billion years old – same old, same old, you might say.

(141)

On the other hand, although our closest celestial neighbor is familiar enough for its physical features to be seen with the naked eye – as evidenced in ancient Greek, Egyptian, and Babylonian images of the lunar surface (Montgomery 11–12) – its visible connection with other stars and planets in space shows how it is part of "the night that was bigger than people and that dated from before their presence on the planet" (Attlee 5).

Yet what connects the past of the moon with potentiality is the way that this temporal removal of the moon from Earth – what Scott Montgomery calls the moon's "purifying distance" (39) – is used as a platform for the staging of the obviously fake. Sometimes this takes quite a blunt form in lunar films, such as the lunar Egyptian architecture seen in *Radar Men from the Moon* (1952); the way that *When Dinosaurs Ruled the Earth* (1970, treatment written by J.G. Ballard) ends with the chronologically incongruous extinction of the dinosaurs, the survival of the human race, and the formation of the moon all taking place concurrently; or the moon-dinosaurs appearing in the upcoming *Iron Sky* sequel, *Iron Sky: The Coming Race* (2016).

At other times, the past is represented in a more abstract manner. In Frances Bodomo's short film *Afronauts* (2014), the real-life attempt of the African Zambia Space Agency to beat the Americans and Russians to the moon is given an obviously aestheticized treatment.[1] In the "Molten Menace" episode of *Radar Men from the Moon*, the past is made concrete in the form of visualizing the primordial soup. Commando Cody (George Wallace) steals an atomic power weapon from the moon men who are now chasing him. Cody hides in a cave and the moon men aim for one of their atomic weapons and the entrance and 'melt' it. A number of special effects sequences done by the Lydecker brothers – and copped from an episode also called "Molten Menace" from *King of the Rocket Men* (1949) – show the melting rock sliding down the screen. The reason this scene is an example of the past of the moon is that such images are reminiscent of the primordial soup out of which life came, a connection which is reinforced in later episodes with other scenes of moltenness on earth, such as volcanos. Like dinosaurs and Attlee's night sky, the primordial soup is an image that came before humanity and is thus, as Ben Woodard puts it in *Slime Dynamics*, a kind of "subtracting meaning, reducing ontological life to biological life," which is "a far more useful weapon in combating a structure than meaning" (66;

Willems 54–6). The structure being fought in *First on the Moon* is the close-down of déjà vu; the way this structure is being fought *Radar Men from the Moon* is foregrounding change in the present through images of the molten potential of the past.

One Million Kingdoms

In another example, Pierre Huyghe's short video *One Million Kingdoms* (2001) also challenges the shutdown of déjà vu by locating potential within a past which did not happen. The video lasts 14 minutes and originally formed part of Huyghe's 2001 Venice Biennale exhibition *Le Château de Turing*. The video came out of a project that Huyghe began planning in the 1990s, based around Jules Verne's novel *Journey to the Center of the Earth*. The project centered on the Snaefellsjökull volcano, near Reykjavik, where the protagonists of Verne's novel begin their descent to the earth's core (Barikin 187). In addition, another use of the site also inspired Huyghe: in 1965 and 1966, NASA used the volcano as a location for training astronauts, including Neil Armstrong and Buzz Aldrin, for their first trip to the moon (ibid.). *One Million Kingdoms* combines both Verne's and NASA's uses of the volcano in order to create another obviously sham picture of the past.

The audio of Huyghe's piece features Neil Armstrong's voice, which is sampled and manipulated in order to narrate a number of points: selections from Verne's novel, part of Armstrong's commentaries on the moon mission, and newly scripted elements. For example, Armstrong is made to narrate: "We are on the threshold, another world, just one small step, we are getting to 1865, at the beginning of chapter 17, it's from here that we should end up at the center of the earth."

Visually, the image of the film includes an anime figure that Huyghe and Philippe Parreno bought the rights for in 1999, named Annlee. She was used in a number of their artworks, along with those of other artists, before being 'retired' in 2002 by having her copyright sold to a foundation which she controlled, thus granting Annlee both her freedom and her death (Barikin 124). In *One Million Kingdoms*, Annlee is made to walk across a lunarscape composed of rising and falling peaks, which are a graphic representation of the sound waves of Armstrong's voice-over.

Like *First on the Moon, One Million Kingdoms* constantly refers to its own artificiality (cf. McDonough 108–10). Annlee is artificial, a digital file purchased for $428 from Kworks, a Japanese firm which develops manga characters for animation houses. The voice-over is also fake, for Neil Armstrong is heard not only reading from *Journey to the Center of the Earth* but also claiming that the reason the astronauts were at the

Snaefellsjökull volcano was to record footage for faking the moon landing. As Paul Hegarty says:

> Part of Huyghe's text even refers to the shooting of moon landings as something fake, so Armstrong gets to undo his own utopian moment, a moment that was conveyed or even created through words (and the residual sounds of communications devices) as much as through the images of men on the moon.

(125)

Both Huyghe's and Fedorchenko's films choose the moon as the location for such shamming. In *First on the Moon*, the moon is a place that was once science fiction and is now a place of fantasy; it is also a figure of the past as seen in the way the primordial soup is represented in the 'moltenness' of *Radar Men from the Moon*. The plasticity of moltenness is also one of the central visual elements of *One Million Kingdoms*, as the entire lunar surface fluctuates along with the fake oscillations of Armstrong's voice. What all of these examples of moon films have in common is that the lunar past is not a plausible past but rather obviously fake. It is from within this tradition of moon films that *First on the Moon* should be located, rather than with *Opération Lune* and other examples of moon-hoax exposés.

Being There

Up to this point, discussion of Fedorchenko's film has focused on a figuration of the potentiality of the past. Paul Virno was used to develop how potentiality is located only in the past because 1) the present is 'ruined' by the ever-increasing sense of déjà vu and 2) an obviously fake past is not the representation of an *old truth* but rather of an alternative possibility. Yet two shots at the end of *First on the Moon* at first seem to turn all of this on its head. The unreality of the film is challenged by two 'actual' images which are shown from the 'real' space flight made by the Soviet cosmonaut. The first image shows Kharlamov ensconced in the rocket and the second shows an incredibly shaky and brief pan on the lunar surface, eventually settling on a lunar lander with CCCP written on it, before the camera violently vibrates and the image disappears.

These images are qualitatively different from the rest of the film. This is supported by their placement at the end, taking place just before the last shot of the cosmonauts stylishly walking away from the camera, as if at the end of a Western.

There is no voice-over for any of these images, indicating that they speak for themselves. And although they are also 'shams,' much of the work of the film is done to make them less fake than all the other images. In this way, they demand an interpretation which takes into account a comparison of these images with the rest of the film.

Initially, it can be said that most of the images in the film are obviously fake while the two being singled out here are obviously (meant to be) real. What are the consequences of this for the argument formed argument, that it is only the fake past which functions as a figure of possibility?

At first, it seems as if *First on the Moon* does little more than follow Siegfried Kracauer's famous dictum that no matter how artificial or artistic a film is that the filmmaker's aesthetic burden lies "in letting nature in and penetrating it" (40). Here, Kracauer rallies against the traditional view that organized cinematic images are somehow antagonistic toward the more natural "camera-reality" captured in the unadulterated film image (39), or what André Bazin describes as the realism of the single image in contradiction to meaning created by the juxtaposition of images in classic montage (26–7). Kracauer, discussing both completely fictive stories such as *Hamlet* and documentary films such as *Nanook of the North* (1922) – although the fictive nature of the latter has long been discussed (Leacock) – is interested in films "which incorporate aspects of physical reality with a view to making us experience them" (Kracauer 40). Following this argument, *First on the Moon* would contain a majority of 'ridiculous' footage in order to make the audience experience a sense of authenticity at the end of the film. Yet this is not what happens in the film at all. Rather than being images of authenticity, the 'real' footage at the end of the film is actually 'doubly-fake' because it is not found footage *and* because it is not an actual event.

Let's clarify this last point, because it is key for understanding how sham ruins can function. For Virno, potential is located in the past because the present is ruined by an overwhelming sense of déjà vu (which arises from an over-awareness of the creation of memory in the present). Yet *First on the Moon* shows that the past is a location of potential only when that past is fake, because it therefore belongs to a 'second' history which does not pretend to be the actual truth but is rather obviously fake. Potentiality is 'fake' because it is a figuration of what has not occurred. Thus, for Virno when the present and future are closed down by déjà vu, it is the past which opens up to potentiality. *First on the Moon* takes this idea one step further. In the film, if the past is now shown to be a location of potentiality, then the present is theoretically freed up for difference. This is what these two strange shots at the end of the film show: a new present freed up by the potentiality of the past. It is in this sense, as Virno says, that "There is no potential that is not, in itself, pre-historic" (184). And this new potential of the present is something which is also not possible, something which is also fake; now there is room for this new present to take place when the constrictions of déjà vu are no longer so tight. Thus, the sham ruin that is *First on the Moon* does two things: it is an alternate history which figures the past as the privileged location of potentiality, and it is a representation of the consequence of such a past, which is the potential for a different present. Thus, the final shot of the film, that of the cosmonauts walking stylishly away from the camera as if at the end of a Western, is apt; they have done their duty and are now going home. This film now functions as a true sham ruin. The present has been gifted to us by the past.

Note

1. Deji Bryce Olukotun's novel *Nigerians in Space* (2014) also utilizes the moon as a sham ruin. In the 1990s, Wale Olufunmi, a lunar geologist from Nigeria living in Houston, Texas, is enticed back to his home country by the mysterious Bello with the promise of setting up a Nigerian space agency and going to the moon himself. Oluktotun later wrote about Olufemi Agboola, a Nigerian émigré engineer who was tasked to set up just an agency (Olukotun). In a more individualistic endeavor, Eugene Awimbo is single-handedly building Kenya's first rocket in his backyard. See: www.facebook.com/eugene_awimbo for updates.

Works Cited

Anderson, Steve. *Technologies of History: Visual Media and the Eccentricity of the Past*. Lebanon: University Press of New England, 2011.

Attlee, James. *Nocturne: A Journey in Search of Moonlight*. Chicago: The University of Chicago Press, 2011.

Augé, Marc. *The Future*. Trans. John Howe. London; New York: Verso Books, 2015.

Bailey, J.O. *Pilgrims through Space and Time: Trends and Patterns in Scientific and Utopian Fiction*. Westport: Greenwood Press, 1972.

Barikin, Amelia. *Parallel Presents: The Art of Pierre Huyghe*. Cambridge: MIT Press, 2012.

Bazin, André. *What Is Cinema?* Trans. Hugh Gray. Vol. 1. Berkeley: University of Los Angeles Press, 1967.

Bergson, Henri. "Memory of the Present and False Recognition." In *Key Writings*. Eds. Keith Ansell Pearson and John Mullarkey. London: Continuum, 2002: 141–56.

Blanchot, Maurice. "The Proper Use of Science Fiction." *Arena*, No. 25/26 (2006): 375–83.

Booker, M. Keith and Anne-Marie Thomas. *The Science Fiction Handbook*. Mladen: Blackwell, 2009.

Brunner, Bernd. *Moon: A Brief History*. New Haven; London: Yale University Press, 2010.

Cooper, Henry S. F. "A Reporter at Large: Men on the Moon (I-Just One Big Rockpile)." *New Yorker* (Apr 12, 1969): 53–90.

Deleuze, Gilles. *Bergsonism*. Trans. Hugh Tomlinson. New York: Zone Books, 1991.

Disch, Thomas. *The Dreams Our Stuff Is Made of: How Science Fiction Conquered the World*. New York: Touchstone, 2000.

Duncan, Andy. "Alternate History." In *The Cambridge Companion to Science Fiction*. Eds. Edward James and Farah Mendlesohn. Cambridge: Cambridge University Press, 2003: 209–18.

Fraser, Rory. *Follies: An Architectural Journey*. London: Zuleika, 2020.

Hegarty, Paul. *Rumour and Radiation: Sound in Video Art*. New York; London: Bloomsbury, 2015.

Hellekson, Karen. *The Alternate History: Refiguring Historical Time*. Kent: Kent State University Press, 2001.

Jameson, Frederic. *The Cultural Turn: Selected Writings on the Postmodern, 1983–1998*. London; New York: Verso, 1998.

Jorgensen, Darren. "States of Weightlessness: Cosmonauts in Film and Television." *Science Fiction Film and Television*, Vol. 2, No. 2 (2009): 205–24.

Kabanova, Daria. "Mourning the Mimesis: Aleksei Fedorchenko's *First on the Moon* and the Post-Soviet Practice of Writing History." *Studies in Slavic Cultures*, Vol. 10 (Oct 2012): 75–93.

Koestler, Arthur. *The Sleepwalkers: A History of Man's Changing Vision of the Universe*. New York: The Universal Library, 1963.

Kovalov, Oleg. "Aleksei Fedorchenko: *First on the Moon* (*Pervye na lune*), 2005." *Review, KinoKultura*, Vol. 11 (2006). Internet: www.kinokultura.com/2006/11r-firstmoon1.shtml.

Kracauer, Siegfried. *Theory of Film: The Redemption of Physical Reality*. New York: Oxford University Press, 1965.

Leacock, Richard. "On Working with Robert and Frances Flaherty." *Academic Film Archive of North America* (Apr 26, 1990). Internet: www.afana.org/leacockessays.htm#On Working With Robert and Frances Flaherty.

Marks, Laura. *Touch: Sensuous Theory and Multisensory Media*. Minneapolis; London: University of Minnesota Press, 2002.

McDonough, Tom. "No Ghost." *October*, Vol. 110 (Autumn 2004): 107–30.

Montgomery, Scott. *The Moon and the Western Imagination*. Tucson: The University of Arizona Press, 1999.

Olukotun, Deji Bryce. "Meeting my Protagonist." *Slate.com* (Sept 19, 2014a). Internet: https://slate.com/technology/2014/09/nigerians-in-space-my-sci-fi-novel-turned-out-to-be-closer-to-the-truth-than-i-expected.html.

Olukotun, Deji Bryce. *Nigerians in Space*. Los Angeles: Unnamed Press, 2014b.

Prokhorov, Alexander. "The Redemption of Lunar Reality: Aleksei Feorchenko's *First on the Moon* (*Pervye na lune*), 2005." *Review, KinoKultura*, Vol. 11 (2006). Internet: www.kinokultura.com/2006/11r-firstmoon2.shtml.

Rebentisch, Juliane. *Aesthetics of Installation Art*. Trans. Daniel Hendrickson and Gerrit Jackson. Berlin: Sternberg Press, 2012.

Rickels, Laurence. *Germany: A Science Fiction*. Fort Wayne: Anti-Oedipal Press, 2015.

Rogatchevski, Andrei. "Space Exploration in Russian and Western Popular Culture: Wishful Thinking, Conspiracy Theories and Other Related Issues." In *Soviet Space Culture: Cosmic Enthusiasm in Socialist Societies*. Eds. Eva Maurer et al. London: Palgrave Macmillan, 2011: 251–65.

Sagan, Carl. *Pale Blue Dot: A Vision of the Human Future in Space*. New York: Random House, 1994.

Scholes, Robert. *Structural Fabulation: An Essay on the Fiction of the Future*. Notre Dame; London: University of Notre Dame Press, 1975.

Shaviro, Steven. *Post Cinematic Affect*. Hants: Zero Books, 2010.

Siddiqi, Asif. "From Cosmic Enthusiasm to Nostalgia for the Fugure: A Tale of Soviet Space Culture." In *Soviet Space Culture: Cosmic Enthusiasm in Socialist Societies*. Eds. Eva Maurer et al. London: Palgrave Macmillan, 2011: 283–306.

Srnick, Nick and Alex Williams. *Inventing the Future: Postcapitalism and a World without Work*. London; New York: Verso, 2015.

Stiegler, Bernard. *Symbolic Misery, Volume 1: The Hyperindustrial Epoch*. Trans. Barnaby Norman. Cambridge; Mladen: Polity Press, 2014.

Vassilieva, Julia. "*First on the Moon*: The Totalitarian Echo in New Russian Cinema." *Rouge*, Vol. 12 (2008). Internet: www.rouge.com.au/12/moon.html.

Virno, Paolo. *Déjà Vu and the End of History*. Trans. David Broder. London; New York: Verso, 2015.

Warf, Barney. "The Way It Wasn't: Alternative Histories, Contingent Geographies." In *Lost in Space: Geographies of Science Fiction*. Eds. Rob Kitchin and James Kneale. London; New York: Continuum, 2002: 17–37.

Willems, Brian. *Shooting the Moon*. Hants: Zero Books, 2015.

Woodard, Ben. *Slime Dynamics*. Hants: Zero Books, 2012.

3 Total Replication

Desiderius Erasmus' *The Praise of Folly* (1511) is generally taken as a joke worked out between the author and Thomas More, as a paradox praising stupidity in learned prose, and as a Lucianic comedy about how the only way people can put up with each other is through the delusion of idiocy. The text is told through its narrator, Folly herself, who is addressing a group of gentleman who have gathered to hear her 'wisdom.' One of the first questions she asks them is how one can ever recognize folly just from its mere appearance:

> Still, what need was there to tell you this, as if in my very face and front, so to speak, I do not sufficiently announce who I am? As if anyone who was claiming that I am Minerva or the Spirit of Wisdom could not immediately be refuted by one good look, even if I were not speaking – though speech is the least deceptive mirror of the mind. I have no use for cosmetics. I do not feign one thing in my face while I hold something else in my heart. I am in all points so like myself that even those who specially arrogate to themselves the part and name of wise men cannot conceal me, though they walk about "like apes in scarlet or asses in lion-skins." Let them carry it as cunningly as you could ask, the protruding ears will somewhere betray the Midas. An ungrateful class of men that, so help me!
>
> (Erasmus 10)

Folly argues that her foolish appearance is so obvious that it is strange that anyone could ever miss it. Someone who might mistake folly for wisdom need to take only "one good look" at her "very face and front" to separate Minerva from an ass. Folly is so recognizable in part because she does not pretend to be anything else, she is "in all points so like myself" that no effort to hide her, even by those pretending to be the wisest, can be successful.

DOI: 10.4324/9781003213086-3

Yet in a satirical work such as Erasmus', a Latin text which chastises authors who insert Greek words just to look smart and yet uses Greek for its own title, Folly's comments should not be taken at face value. They should be read as saying the opposite, actually. Folly is at times indistinguishable from wisdom, either because it is so well hidden by those who want to be taken as wise, or because it has no obvious markers. Hence, the need for Erasmus' text, elaborating many different kinds of folly which might not seem obvious to the reader at first, becomes visible through the medium of satire.

In the previous chapters, sham ruins were also, at times, confused for real ones. In Chapter 1, Rose Macaulay was quoted asking "How can one tell?" (16) if a ruin from the past is a sham ruin or not, since over time sham ruins also decay, eventually becoming indistinguishable from 'authentic' ones because they have become real ruins themselves. And in the second chapter, Aleksei Fedorchenko's mockumentary *First on the Moon* was confused for a real documentary film, winning the 2005 Venice Horizons Documentary Award, despite not being a documentary at all. This chapter also focuses on an example of a sham ruin of sorts and one which is purposely created to be a replication of its original, although this example is from the world of art rather than architecture, literature, or film. The artist Sturtevant took the work of mainly male artists and, even using some of the same materials and equipment at times, made replications that for all intents and purposes were replicas of the originals, except that they were by Sturtevant and not Warhol or Lichtenstein. These 'copies' are not forgeries since they do not pretend to be the originals. And yet they expressly do not function as the originals, and that is their point.

Sturtevant

There are a number of reasons not to include Sturtevant in a discussion of sham ruins. A sham ruin is a trick. A ruse. A con. Sturtevant's work is none of these. Even though her art often looks very similar to the original, there is no pretension to 'pretend' that it is anything other than it is: a replication of someone else's work of art by the artist Sturtevant. Therefore, a piece by Warhol called *Flowers* is called *Warhol's Flowers* in Sturtevant's hands. Sturtevant's work does not pretend to be Warhol's work. If it did, it would lose all its meaning.

Yet there are important connections between Sturtevant and the way sham ruins are being used in this book. Most of her work looks like an original work by another artist, and yet it is not, just as sham ruins look like real ruins, and yet they are not. More importantly, Sturtevant's work *functions* like sham ruins function. Ruins are not sham ruins because real ruins were built as actual, valid, useful structures that then decayed over time. Real ruins do not start out as ruins, they start out as something else, and external forces, whether natural or human-made, turn this something else into a ruin. Sham ruins are different. They are ruins from the start, so that even if over time they turn into 'real' ones, the original that is ruined is still a fake, although admittedly an original fake.

Yet something else gets ruined with sham ruins, and if it is not the original that gets ruined, then what is it? Sturtevant's work offers a clue. Seeing her art as ruining the originals she replicates is a mistake. If she really wanted to ruin Warhol's original *Flowers*, she could have made exact copies of the work (which she actually could have done since she had access to Warhol's original silk screens)[1] and then tried to 'mix' her copies in with the originals, thus devaluing the original status of the work (somewhat akin to Warhol's own artistic strategy). But she does not do that. She does not aim to ruin the original work. Her goal is something much more important than that, because she casts a much wider net.

Therefore, this chapter centers on what the sham ruins of Sturtevant ruin. Of course, these are not sham ruins in the architectural sense but in an artistic one. Just as Fedorchenko's film was argued to be a sham ruin because of the way it falsified a history that never happened, Sturtevant's work replicates the work of another artist to such a degree that once again the following question is raised: what do sham ruins ruin? One answer to this question from the previous chapters was truth, while here the answer will be themselves. This new answer is hinted at by Erasmus's Folly, who is "in all points so like myself," yet easily confused with wisdom. The work of Sturtevant is also in all points so like itself that it immediately addresses that which it is not, thus "plunging right into the Bermuda Triangle of idea, method, and execution" (Heiser 248).

Yet Sturtevant is not the only example of 'sham ruin art.' In Chapter 2, Pierre Huyghe's video *One Million Kingdoms* was seen to make no attempt to hide the way it turns the moon landing into a sham, and other work follows a similar pattern. In 2007, once-schoolmates Edgar Arceneaux, Vincent Galen Johnson, Olga Koumoundouros, Rodney McMillian, and Matthew Sloly reimagined Constantin Brâncuși's *Endless Column* (1926), a tall construction mainly built out of repeated rhomboids. The contemporary artists made the column look like it had been rammed through the various floors of Harlem's Studio Museum. The result was a broken *Endless Column* that was obviously not the original. There was no pretension that the original had been transported from Romania and then destroyed to make this piece (say in the way Ai Weiwei destroyed a real million-dollar Han Dynasty urn in 1995), yet this obvious fakeness was no detriment to the fact that a piece of art had been made (Williams 94).

The Harlem Studio Museum piece is called *Philosophy of Time Travel*, a title taken from a fictional book that appears in the film *Donny Darko* (2001). In the movie, the book is a product of Roberta Sparro, also known as Grandma Death, an elderly woman who is perpetually waiting for a letter that never arrives. The movie itself develops a number of different time-lines, indicating that the artists are, if nothing else, like Huyghe, interested in the way their work ruins time, although in this example it takes place in the reformulation of Brâncuși's work.

The original *Endless Column* is itself a bit of a time warp. It was first exhibited in New York in 1926, when the date of its composition was given as 1918, although at times it was thought to have been conceived as early as 1909, although this is no longer accepted (Geist 71–2). Even the name of the work is unstable, having been called *Column Without End* in a 1933–4 exhibition at the NYC Brummer Gallery (although in the exhibition catalog it was referred to as "Endless Columns"), while in French the work is called either *Colonne sans fin* or *Colonne infinie* (80–1). And the meaning of the work also changed over the many different versions Brâncuși make of it over the years, starting from references to African Sculpture to functioning as a memorial to Romanian soldiers who died in the First World War, prompting Sidney Geist to state that "its significance seems to have changed with the occasion that called it forth" (87), thus 'ruining' whatever meaning the sculpture had previously held.

But the column is more directly ruined in the Harlem Studio exhibition, in which the work is actually broken into pieces as it thrusts through ceilings on each floor, with remnants and debris spread throughout. The force that has caused this destruction is unclear, unless the exhibition title, *Philosophy of Time*, indicates that something has shifted the sculpture from the past into the present. Due to the golden color of the sculpture (rather than being in mere wood), as well as its height of about 100 feet, it is assumed that the version of the work the artists used as inspiration is based on the last and most famous one Brâncuși completed, the 1938 memorial edition installed at Târgu Jiu. However, another option could be considered: before his death, Brâncuși was thinking about an even larger column, of 1,665 feet, which at the time would have been the tallest structure in the world, and which was originally planned for New York City (ibid.). Yet whatever the version, *Philosophy of Time* repurposes Brâncuși's work by ruining it, a classic sham ruins technique.[2]

Obvious and Less Obvious

Other examples of the use of the purposely broken can be found in much of the work of Croatian conceptual artist Momčilo Golub. His work often involves retooling found objects by breaking them into new uses and combinations. For example, chevrons are ripped off a uniform and hung next to a rabbit pelt on the wall, or a cello is covered with raw wool, making it unplayable. In another piece, a number of cheap porcelain teapots, cups, and saucers have been smashed and then strung up together from a gallery ceiling. Yet what 'ruins' these objects is not so much the smashing but rather the name the artist has given the piece. *The Porcelain Poem Claps its Hands, While the Crushed Begs and Dies/Porculanska pjesma plješće rukama, zatim zdrobljena prosi i umire*, rips the smashed porcelain out of any possible function it might have been assigned by the viewer and puts them fully in the hands of the artist. This is what Peli Grietzer calls *poetry*, meaning the connection between an object's manifest image (its social function) and its scientific image (materiality) (Grietzer). What has broken the objects is not so much the hands of the artist but rather the 'poetic' meaning he assigns them, thus making their obviously cracked and broken surfaces merely the manifestation of the nonfunctionality assigned by the title.

These artworks are used to show how not all sham ruin art is hard to spot. Yet other examples attempt to hide their fake nature. Some follow Erasmus's Folly in trying to conceal their foolishness under the guise of wisdom. For example, in the summer of 2009, *The New York Times* ran a story called "The Ruins of the Gilded Age." The online version of the article featured a slide show with a number of photographs of contemporary ruins, including abandoned factories and ghost towns. The article has since been taken down. This is because Edgar Martins, the photographer of the images used, used Photoshop to make the images look more ruined than they actually did in real life (Dunlap). It is these manipulated photographs which form contemporary sham ruins, not the ruins featured in the story. This is because the Photoshopped pictures ruin truth. For, as Martins stated in an article, he wrote after the story was redacted (although he has also removed this essay from his personal website), "the strength of the work resides precisely in the illusion of photographic transparency" (cited in Beesley). The 'truth' that this sham ruin indicates is the desire for objects to look destitute being greater than the destitution of the objects themselves.

This is an example of a rather underhanded use of sham ruins, mainly because sham ruins can so easily be confused with real ones. Yet some artists also use this confusion as a theme of their work. In 1966, Yoko Ono exhibited *Play It By Trust* in which all the pieces of a chess set, as well as the board, were painted the same shade of white. If any players actually started a game using this board, once their all-white pieces started to mix, the game, unless the players had a very high level of concentration,[3] would quickly stop, or at least turn into a nonstandard game of chess. This is because the two sides would become indistinguishable. The standard rules of play would no longer apply. This means either the game would have to be abandoned or new rules would have to be devised. Based on the title of the piece, these rules would have to be based on trust rather than competition, thus fitting into the anti-war theme of the piece.

Ono's work indicates a new function of sham ruins, which is actually a kind of anti-function, or anti-play. The white chess set engages with the rules of the game only to upend them.

Yet this does not quite mean game over for Ono's piece. In this work, it is not that a game cannot be played, but rather that the intended game has been ruined in order for another one to take its place. In *Critical Play: Radical Game Design*, Mary Flanagan describes this shift in this work and others from Ono:

> Using everyday items like chess pieces, game boards, or scissors, Ono allows participants in the work to consider the marvelous nature of the everyday and engage with game-like concepts and processes in an endless queue of provocative situations. *Play It By Trust* emphasizes the ways in which serious issues might be tackled through games, and how multiple participants in games have equal opportunities and face equal stakes. Reskinning, or painting the work all white, eliminates the element of competition from the traditional form of the game.
>
> (113)

Flanagan uses Ono's work to develop her concept of *unplaying*, which, in the case of children using dolls for the unexpected uses of killing or other abuse, "specifically enact 'forbidden' or secret scenes, unfortunate scenarios, or other unanticipated conclusions often in opposition to an acceptable or expected adult-play script" (33). Ono's chessboard demands that its players unplay chess. This does not mean that they stop playing, but rather that they have to play something else, something unplanned.[4]

Knowledge Is Made for Cutting

The basic definition of sham ruins used in this book is the objects that are purposely dysfunctional. The task of this book is then to develop the novel ways they are used. The broken Brâncuşi column purposely does not work as its intended purpose (or at least one of them, which is itself disruptive): a WWI memorial, just as Ono's chessboard intentionally frustrates any players foolish enough to use it for a standard game. The artist Sturtevant is included in this discussion because she also makes objects that purposely do not work, however, they do not work in a very specific way. They actually combine the two types of sham ruin art that have been discussed so far in this chapter. First, we discussed art which was obviously a sham and then some art that was not. Sturtevant's work is both at once. She makes replications of existing artworks that are as close as possible to the original. She shows, in her own words, "the brutal truth of the work that is not a copy" (qtd. in Lee, Patricia 21). For example, when making one of her most famous pieces, based on Warhol's *Flowers* (1964), she asked the artist if she could use his original printing screens and he agreed (Heiser 248). This was done to make her work as indistinguishable as possible from the model. Yet she never actually pretended that her work was that of the original artist. Sturtevant called her work *Warhol Flowers* (1968) and had no intent to plagiarize the artist's work or to pass it off as her own.[5] The reason for her work was found elsewhere. Using the concept of sham ruins, this 'elsewhere' will come into focus.

In an essay originally presented at one of the Tate Modern Saturday Live events in 2009, Sturtevant discusses some of the key concepts and approaches of her work. The essay is called "Modes of Thought," and it quickly features a phrase that is paramount for understanding just how her work can be considered under the rubric of sham ruins. After stating how "Repetition is displaced difference" and "Repetition is pushing the limits of resemblance," the artist says that "Understanding is not the role of knowledge, rather knowledge is made for cutting, this is indeed my premise" (Sturtevant). What is the 'cut' that Sturtevant mentions in this quote when her work functions as a mode of replication? No matter whether or not one can differentiate her work from the original, the cut does not lie in the quality of her images. Rather the cut is to be found in the difference between Warhol as creator and Sturtevant as creator. And since many of her images were made before the original artists became famous, this cut is not just about a more famous and less famous artist making the same work. Nor is this is a cut merely made along the lines of sex, although Sturtevant has mainly made copies of male artists' work, whether they be famous or yet-to-be famous, and so the 'knowledge' that is made for cutting could be argued to be a knowledge of the sex of the artist and the assumed reception such an artist could expect in distinction to the reception a woman of the same talent and creating the same work could look forward to, a kind of Shakespeare's sister of the art world.

Yet these lines of thought lead us to another kind of cut, the physical and bloody kind. As reported in a *World Journal Tribune* article of 1967, the day before the opening of Sturtevant's exhibition *The Store of Claes Oldenburg*, in which she repeated the Pop artist's 'store' from a few years earlier, the artist was violently attacked. She "was treated at New York Hospital for cuts and bruises on her body and head" (qtd. in Hainley 22), although she was not attacked by any budding Pop art purists, but rather "a pack of

300 school children between the ages of 8 and 16, while shopkeepers and passersby stood around and watched without so much as a blink of an eye" (ibid.). Yet this was not a random attack. Kids from a local school had been hanging around all week while Sturtevant was putting up the exhibition, "standing in front of the store, cracking jokes, shouting abusive language and, finally, putting firecrackers through the mail slot, and forcing the door open, even though I kept it locked" (24). And theirs was not the only attack of the day:

> By 4 o'clock, most of the kids had gone. I thought I would be safe to leave the store and go home. I walked out and began crossing Tompkins Square. I suddenly felt someone following me, and then I felt someone grabbing my arm again. There were two men and a woman. They pushed me down on a bench. The two men held my arms back, while the woman broke a bottle over my head.
>
> (ibid.)

We can assume that the attackers were not a brood of young Claes Oldenburg collectors who were out to protect their investment from a potential forger. We can also assume that, perhaps, they did not exactly know what Sturtevant was doing, at least in the sense of replication. But they knew something was wrong. Something was being attacked and something had to be defended. And to do this they did not attack the work, but the artist. If knowledge is made for cutting, then the way to stop knowledge is also to cut. The attacks on Sturtevant show exactly where the target of her own work lies: not in the work but rather in the culture of reception.

[sic]

The report of this event is taken from Bruce Hainley's book *Under the Sign of [sic]: Sturtevant's Volte-Face* (2013).[6] Hainley is one of the leading experts on Sturtevant's art (if not the), and his book offers some of the definitive insights into the artist's life and work. Two key terms for understanding Hainley's reading come from the title of the book itself: [sic] and volte-face. When used in square brackets, [*sic*] denotes editorial intervention into a cited text. In full meaning *sic erat scriptum*, or *thus it was written*, [sic] denotes that an author is aware that the words they are using contain an error, but that they have been transcribed verbatim, warts, and all. Thus, the term incorporates both replication and error, a fitting combination for Sturtevant's work. However, the question remains, what is the error that her work foregrounds?

Hainley is not very helpful on this point, at least from the perspective of thinking about the inappropriate uses of sham ruins. His book on the artist is full of historical material, and he has peppered it with [sic]s when he has found issues with the archive. As he has said in an interview in the *Los Angeles Review of Books*:

> By tracking early-ish Sturtevantian goings-on as diligently as possible, then marking all the discrepancies I found in the historical record with a '[*sic*],' I hope reading the book psyches out what is taken to be 'absent' or 'present,' 'serious' or 'beneath consideration,' 'now' or 'then.' We see only what we are able or wish to, which doesn't make what we see what was or, even, what is.

(Durbin)

If the error that [*sic*] makes visible is that which is taken to be absent, or present, or serious, or not serious, or now, nor then, it is not very helpful. When taken at face value, this list is too general to be useful. But of course Hainley is not meaning to be taken at face value. Instead, he seems to be indirectly indicating the second term of his book title, volte-face, which simply means about-face or, more colloquially, to make a U-turn. This list from the interview can then be read as a series of such U-turns, in fact indicating that it is the U-turn itself that is important for Sturtevant's work rather than the actual items being U-turned.[7]

The volte-face is a useful concept for reading Sturtevant's work, but for the purposes of sham ruins, [*sic*] is much more important. Sham ruins are not an about-face. They are not 'up,' while real ruins are 'down.' The relationship between sham ruins and real ones is not that of opposition, and I do not even think Sturtevant's relationship to the work she replicates, or even to the artists that created the original work, is one of opposition either. Operating under the sign of [*sic*] is different. With [*sic*], a timeline is created, stretching from the original author to the one who corrects. A sense of judgment is created, placing one person in the position of knowing less and the other of knowing more. And most importantly, an intervention is created, with the square brackets allowing the contemporary author to insert their voice directly into the actual text of what they are quoting, interrupting the original author from another time and space, jumping into their language, rather than being regulated to the sidelines of commenting either before or after the text that is quoted.

This last feature of [*sic*], meaning the actual introjection of one author into another's work, is where Sturtevant and sham ruins have the most intimate connection. Sham ruins are essentially decorations for the gardens

of the rich. Thus, they are found outdoors and have been taken to be inter-
jections of art into nature, of the "projection of art into Nature" (Logan
Pearsall Smith quotes in Clark 47). Yet the manner in which this introjection takes place needs clarification. Sturtevant's work is not about a single
one of her pieces, nor is it about a single piece from a single artist that
she replicates; her work is rather about what she calls the "total structure"
(Hainley and Lobel 117) of a work of art. This means that her replications do not just address the surface of the work, nor the artist himself,
nor merely the context of reception or production, nor simply the politics
of acquisition, archive, and exhibition. Rather her work addresses all of
these aspects at the same time, and more. As Sturtevant has said herself,
"So the power behind the work is that it always has to be presented as a
totality, not as individual pieces, otherwise they are just wrecks – they're
gone" (ibid.). Although the term "wrecks" could function as a tempting
distraction in the context of ruins, we should not get sidelined here from
the artist's main point. Sturtevant started using the term "total structure"
in the late 1960s. One of the main ways she uses this term is to encompass
a comprehensive critique of the art world, and this critique is meant to
"trigger thinking" (125) in her viewers. Thus, in the words of Peter Eleey,
her work should not be viewed piece-by-piece, but rather, "the radicalness
of what she proposed, crucially, depends as much upon the duration and
steadfastness of her commitment . . . as it does upon the apparent ease of
its gesture, enacted at full scale" (53).

Yet at first the [*sic*] seems to be a poor framework for such a total structure since it takes aim at the minute of spelling, misnaming, and typos. In
other words, just as Sturtevant's work is not about the individual object,
perhaps the [sic] can be retooled into a more general concept for addressing a total structure. As I have set out elsewhere (Willems 52–5), ever since
Jean-François Lyotard at least, any discussion of totalizing structures seems
suspicious. In *The Postmodern Condition*, Lyotard calls total structures
grand narratives, which are meta stories used to legitimize and natural-
ize the actions of specific cultures (38). Lyotard's aim is to denaturalize
these narratives and instead foreground local narratives, meaning narratives
"agreed on by its present players and subject to eventual cancellation" (66).
While Lyotard's work has rightfully had much influence, in the current age
of globalization and rampant neoliberalism, global problems need global
solutions rather than just local potshots.

The Invisible Committee's *To Our Friends* is a text that takes the local
to task and foregrounds the need for thinking globally. In fact, it does more
than this: it sees the global in local terms, which then has the consequence of
making what seems too big to change manageable. Its anonymous author(s),

believed to include Julien Coupat, the anarchist convicted of sabotaging the French high-speed train network in 2008, argue(s) that:

> We risk losing everything if we invoke the local as against the global. The local is not the reassuring alternative to globalization, but its universal product. Before the world was globalized, the place I inhabit was simply my familiar territory – I didn't think of it as 'local.' Local is just the underside of global, its residue, its secretion, and not something capable of shattering it.
>
> (188)

The Invisible Committee argues that the universal is a concrete entity, tied to actual institutions, processes, abstract ideas, and people, and all of these are open to change. This line of thinking is close to that of Nick Srnicek and Alex Williams, who also focus on changing the global once it becomes localized. They develop a concept to describe this possibility for change that is quite in line with Sturtevant's thought, and that is the idea of a "subversive universal" (Srnicek and Williams 75–8), which functions as an:

> empty placeholder that hegemonic particulars (specific demands, ideals and collectives) come to occupy. It can operate as a subversive and emancipatory vector of change with respect to established universalists, and it is heterogeneous and includes differences, rather than eliminating them.
>
> (78)

One important aspect of The Invisible Committee and Srnicek and Williams is the way they envision the incorporation of individual entities, objects, and processes into the universal. Thus, we do not need to see this universalization as a turning away from objects themselves. In a similar manner, Sturtevant separated herself from conceptual artists because of her concern for objects in distinction to pure language (Hainley and Lobel 118),[8] and in order to agree with Eleey's comment that "as art has shifted its meaning from *the object* out toward broader networks, dispersed horizontally into the 'total structure' that concerned Sturtevant" (70), we have to adopt a rather limited idea of what an object is.

Sturtevant does not ruin the original she replicates because she does not take aim at any single aspect of an artwork or artist. Rather she is interested in questioning *everything* involved in the artwork, including issues of production, reception, exhibition, and archiving. "I have no place at all except in relation to the total structure," she said, "What interests me is not communicating but creating change" ("Trends" 71). And this total change can be disturbing. In the words of Anne Dressen:

> Sturtevant is intransigent, wily, cannibalistic. She annoys as much as she ravishes, in every sense of the word. Far from being a matter of distanced, allusive quotation, her entire practice is more suggestive of performance. And the violence present at the very outset has become more obvious in her recent work.
>
> (17)

This is a description of not only Sturtevant's work but also sham ruins at their best, as intransigent and cannibalistic, ravishing and annoying. The question then becomes how such replications become so powerful. Part of the reason is that they redefine the notion of an object itself.

Objects and Wholes

In order to develop this new concept of the object, we will first turn to the work of Graham Harman, who provided the idea of 'ruination' used in the first chapter of this book. In *Art and Objects*, Harman makes an argument for art as a "self-contained object" (x), meaning that "Art is autonomous for the same reason as everything else: however significant the relations between one field or object and another, most things do not affect each other in the least" (xi). What Harman means here is that objects exist outside of their relations to one another. A pen's interaction with paper does not exhaust all of the possible relations paper can have to other objects. Paper's relation to fire is different, as is paper's relation to a shredding machine. In fact, the possible relations paper can have to different objects never exhausts what paper is. There is always something left over, something withdrawn. This is what Harman means by "most things do not affect each other in the least," in that very often the manner an object does not relate to others is more important than the relations it does have.

Hence, the importance of Sturtevant's "total structure": nothing escapes it. She aims at every relation a work of art can have. Not just social, or gendered, or classist. But all of it. That is why she needs to replicate the whole artwork. In order to try and capture all of its relations. And that is why there needs to be a difference between her work and the one she replicates, to engender thinking about these relations.

However, this does not mean that Sturtevant's work is staking a claim to any kind of 'whole.' Nor does it try and destroy such a whole. Rather, it roots at the ground underneath the replicated work's feet by showing that such a whole was never possible. By this I mean that her work does not attack any individual element of another work, nor does it even try and disrupt a system. Rather her work, by replicating another, yet with difference, is, following a similar trajectory to that of Pamela Lee, "forgetting the art world," which is not "to leave it behind as though stepping outside it, but to acknowledge both its ubiquity and the continuity of its techniques with a world that we once thought it surveyed, as if existing 'down below'" (186).

In *The Democracy of Objects*, Levi Bryant makes a similar argument when he says:

> If it is to be established that the World does not exist, then what is required is not a demonstration of the *possibility* of the ruin of any Whole, but rather the demonstration that *in fact* the World does not exist.
>
> (274)

Put briefly, the World here is similar to what Harman means when he talks about the relations an object has with another which are never exhausted. When Bryant says the World does not exist here, he does not mean we are living in some kind of virtual reality, but rather, just as how the paper's relations to a pen do not express all of the paper's possible relations, the World does not exist because the openness of one object to another "is always of a selective nature" (ibid.). Self-contained objects, forgetting the art world, and the fact that the World itself does not exist, all point to the same thing: objects are more than their relation to other objects. There is something that always remains withdrawn, hidden from view. And here we come back to Sturtevant. Back to why she makes replications and not copies. Copies are exact, while her replications introduce difference. This difference is what is being called the withdrawn characteristic of objects. It is what her work brings forth:

> Replication is a breath-taking
> conceptual idea that has greatly
> pushed the limitation of resemblance;
> holding the higher powers of
> non-identity and difference.
> . . .
> Repeating might be an
> excellent mode for replicating,
> but it is back to the surface again.
> It desperately cares what it
> "looks like" rather than
> containing silent power,
> which is of no interest.
>
> (Sturtevant 9)

Notes

1. Warhol's silkscreens are not the only example of Sturtevant replicating the technique of those she repeated. For example, in "Inherent Vice or Vice Versa," she describes the difficulty in getting the same black paint Frank Stella used (she had to find not a store carrying old black paint, but a store with an owner who knew someone in Brooklyn who had a basement full of old black paint, "But that is a throw of the dice") and she drove the manufacturer and chemist "totally crazy" trying to find the same scull-metal lightbulbs used by Jasper Johns (Sturtevant 33), yet this should not be used as evidence that Sturtevant was making an exact copy but rather was searching for the exact right aspect of the work in which to insert difference.
2. Another connection with *Donnie Darko* could be made in how the main character, a high school student, seems to be the only one to understand the meaning of a homework assignment, reading Graham Greene's short story "The Destructors" (1954), in which a group of kids purposely destroy a house, simply because it is beautiful (amid the surrounding bombed-out ruins from the Second World War), burning the money they find inside it because robbery is not the point, destruction is (Green).
3. Next to the chessboard, Ono placed a placard reading "CHESS SET FOR PLAYING AS LONG AS YOU CAN REMEMBER WHERE ALL YOUR PIECES ARE."
4. In *Play Anything*, Ian Bogost disagrees with this interpretation, seeing Ono's chessboard as reinforcing the "flexibility and resilience" (105–6) of the original game, working more as a piece of irony than anything subversive: "White Chess Set undermines neither chess nor war; mostly it succeeds as a static sculpture created by a famous artist" (106–7).
5. Warhol himself had many legal issues regarding the images he 'borrowed,' including the photo of hibiscus flowers taken by Patricia Caulfield used for *Flowers*. Caulfield sued and the two settled out of court (Lee 17).
6. This material was previously included in Hainley's 2011 essay "Store as Cunt" which focuses on the Oldenburg replication (Hainley).
7. The fact that the U-turn should be taken as a key concept for reading Hainley's book as a whole is indicated in the book's design, in which Sturtevant's *Haring Tag* (1986) appears on the cover without any text, and the book must literally be turned over in order to read the title and author.
8. This quote is from an edited conversation held between Bruce Hainley, Michael Lobel, and Sturtevant. In the original, unedited transcript, Sturtevant puts even more emphasis on the difference between conceptual thinking and conceptual artists. She is responding to a comment during a talk she gave in Berlin in which she was asked if she was a conceptual artist. Her response was "are you talking about conceptual thinking, or are you identifying as conceptual artist" (Hainley and Lobel 44). When he emphasized that, he meant artist Sturtevant disagrees, implying that her idea of total structures is about conceptual thinking but not conceptual art.

Works Cited

———. "Trends: Statements in Paint." *Time*, Vol. 93, No. 9 (Feb 28, 1969). Internet: http://content.time.com/time/subscriber/article/0,33009,900703-3,00.html.

Beesley, Ruby. "This Is Not a House." *Aesthetica* (2012). Internet: www.aesthetica-magazine.com/this-is-not-a-house/.

Bogost, Ian. *Play Anything: The Pleasure of Limits, the Uses of Boredom, and the Secret of Games*. New York: Basic Books, 2016.

Bryant, Levi. *The Democracy of Objects*. Ann Arbor: Open Humanities Press, 2011.

Clark, Kenneth. *The Gothic Revival: An Essay in the History of Taste*. New York: Harper & Row, 1972.

Dressen, Anne. "Sturtevant's Fake Mirages." In *Sturtevant: The Razzle Dazzle of Thinking*. Ed. Anne Dressen. Paris: ARC/Musée d'Art moderne de la Ville de Paris, 2010: 17–28.

Dunlap, David. "Behind the Scenes: Edgar Martins Speaks." *New York Times* (Jul 31, 2009). Internet: http://lens.blogs.nytimes.com/2009/07/31/behind-10/?_r=0.

Durbin, Andrew. "Unhinged in the Jetztzeit: An Interview with Bruce Hainley." *Los Angeles Review of Books* (Mar 18, 2014). Internet: https://lareviewofbooks.org/article/unhinged-jetztzeit-interview-bruce-hainley/.

Eleey, Peter. "Dangerous Concealment: The Art of Sturtevant." In *Sturtevant: Double Trouble*. Ed. Peter Eleey. New York: MOMA, 2014: 47–78.

Erasmus, Desiderius. *The Praise of Folly*. Trans. Hoyt Hopewell Hudson. Princeton: Princeton University Press, 2015.

Flanagan, Mary. *Critical Play: Radical Game Design*. Cambridge: MIT Press, 2009.

Geist, Sidney. "Brancusi: The 'Endless Column'." *Art Institute of Chicago Museum Studies*, Vol. 16, No. 1 (1990): 70–87; 95.

Greene, Graham. *Complete Short Stories*. London: Penguin, 2005.

Grietzer, Peli. *Big Mood: A Transcendental-Computational Essay on Art*. Forthcoming.

Hainley, Bruce. "Store as Cunt." *Art Journal*, Vol. 70, No. 4 (2011): 84–109.

Hainley, Bruce. *Under the Sign of [sic]: Sturtevant's Volte-Face*. Los Angeles: Semiotext(e), 2013.

Hainley, Bruce and Michael Lobel. "Oral History Interview with Elaine Sturtevant, 2007 July 25–26." *Smithsonian Archives of American Art* (2007). Internet: www.aaa.si.edu/download_pdf_transcript/ajax?record_id=edanmdm-AAADCD_oh_271790.

Hainley, Bruce and Michael Lobel. "Sturtevant in Conversation with Bruce Hainley and Michael Lobel." In *Sturtevant: Double Trouble*. Ed. Peter Eleey. New York: MOMA, 2014: 115–27.

Harman, Graham. *Art and Objects*. Cambridge: Polity Press, 2020.

Heiser, Jörg. *All of a Sudden: Things That Matter in Contemporary Art*. Trans. Nicholas Grindell. Berlin: Sternberg Press, 2008.

Invisible Committee, The. *To Our Friends*. Trans. Robert Hurley. South Pasadena: Semiotext(e), 2015.

Lee, Pamela. *Forgetting the Art World*. Cambridge: MIT Press, 2012.

Lee, Patricia. *Sturtevant: Warhol Marilyn*. London: Afterall Books, 2016.

Lyotard, Jean-François. *The Postmodern Condition: A Report on Knowledge*. Trans. Geoff Bennington and Brian Massumi. Minneapolis; London: University of Minnesota Press, 1984.

Macaulay, Rose. *Pleasure of Ruins*. New York: Walker and Col., 1966.

Srnicek, Nick and Alex Williams. *Inventing the Future: Postcapitalism and a World Without Work*. London; New York: Verso, 2015.

Sturtevant. "Inherent Vice or Vice Versa." In *Sturtevant: The Razzle Dazzle of Thinking*. Ed. Anne Dressen. Paris: ARC/Musée d'Art moderne de la Ville de Paris, 2010: 29–33.

Sturtevant. "Modes of Thought." *Tate Modern* (Feb 19, 2009). Internet: www.tate.org.uk/context-comment/audio/ubs-openings-saturday-live-sturtevant-modes-thought.

Willems, Brian. "Things That Go Nowhere: Scale, City and the List in Richard Price's *Lush Life*." *Umjetnost riječi*, Vol. 62, No. 1 (2018): 51–70.

Williams, Gilda. "It Was What It Was: Modern Ruins." In *Ruins*. Ed. Brian Dillon. London: Whitechapel Gallery Ventures Limited; Cambridge: MIT Press, 2011: 94–9.

4   Homes on Fire

The loss of home is a traumatic event. In Alain Mabanckou's novel *Black Moses* (2015), the main character Moses is orphaned as a baby and struggles to make a home with his caretakers. Taking place in 1970s Congo-Brazzaville, after the rise of the Marxist-Leninist regime a number of changes are made to the orphanage staff, causing the situation to become even more unbearable. So at the age of 13 Moses runs away to the nearby (then) capital Pointe-Noire. After spending some years as a petty criminal in a street gang, Moses, for the first time in his life, finds a home in the shape of a brothel, run by Maman Fiat 500 (nicknamed after a gift she received from one of her clients). Taken in by Maman and tasked to do small tasks for the sex workers and their clients, Moses has finally found a family he loves. Yet when the city's Mayor makes his new re-election slogan "Zero Zairian whores in Pointe-Noire" (Maman is from Zaire, and the Mayor is angry she has other clients than himself), the sex workers are murdered, and the brothel is razed to the ground. Moses loses not only his family and home but seemingly, also his mind. The manner in which he 'loses his mind' is quite peculiar, and it has consequences for a discussion of putting sham ruins to new and unexpected use.[1]

The Adverbials of *Black Moses*

Moses loses his mind when he loses the use of adverbials. This is manifest in how he stops making obvious sense to most people. His responses no longer match the context of his conversations. For example, when asked about his most recent memory, he responds that it is of gnomes in his garden. When asked if he might have been mistaken the gnomes for some of his friends, he says no:

> They had mouths, arms, noses, ears and something dangling down between their legs, if you know what I mean. There were lots of them.

DOI: 10.4324/9781003213086-4

One of them, the oldest, I think, was dressed as a customs officer and was talking about having to feed his ten children and nephews.

(Mabanckou 173)

This story is told to a psychologist that a friend of Moses takes him to. During their sessions together Moses rejects various diagnoses and offers one of his own in their place. "I'm ill because of my adverbials . . ." (171). When asked by the psychologist to explain what he means, Moses says:

My friend Strong-as-Death told me that the purpose of the adverbial is to complete the action expressed by the verb, according to the circumstances in which it is undertaken. Which means, if I'm not mistaken, that without it, the verb is fucked, it can't express cause, means or comparison etc. with any degree of precision. Perhaps my memory is no longer reliable because I've lost most of my adverbials! Or maybe I don't know where to put them in my sentences! If my adverbials aren't there when I need them, I won't be able to remember the time, place or manner etc., and my verbs will be all alone, they'll be orphans like me, which means I'm getting no information about the circumstances of the actions I perform. Strong-as-Death thinks I could pick up some adverbials in the street, because some people just throw them away when they've used them, but I'd need to pick up some that correspond to the ones I've lost. Which would be difficult, because I'm not the only person looking for them in this town and even when I find one, it never seems to be the same as I had before, so I.

(ibid.)

The loss of Moses' home causes him to lose his adverbials. Adverbials are different from adverbs. They are not different words per se, but rather they have a different function. All adverbials are adverbs, although the reverse is not true. Adverbs modify a verb, while adverbials have a more totalizing function, as they modify a whole clause, phrase, or sentence. Therefore, in "She talks quickly," *quickly* is an adverb since it modifies the way she talks, while in "She talks quickly when she's nervous," *when she's nervous* is an adverbial since it modifies not only the verb *talks* but also the whole phrase *She talks quickly*. Thus, an adverbial is a mechanism "whereby one clause can be said to modify another in a way similar to the way in which an adverb modifies a proposition" (Thompson, Longacre, and Hwang 237).

With the loss of his adverbials, Moses does not just have issues with individual words or meanings, but rather with the whole context of his existence. Adverbials, much like Sturtevant's total structure discussed in the previous chapter, cast a wide net. Just as Sturtevant's work is never aimed at an individual painting, adverbials are not aimed at individual words, but rather whole clauses, groups of words, and whole phrases. Moses' psychologist of course will hear none of this and terminates their sessions. He wants nothing to do with explaining psychological states using grammatical structures. Yet Moses insists. Therefore, to understand better the power of Moses' description of his illness, we should take a closer look at the quote previously and see some of the specific elements and forces that it mentions.

If we break down the quote into its component parts, we find that a number of characteristics of adverbials are described:

> to *complete* the action expressed by the verb
> adverbials define *the circumstances* in which an action is undertaken
> without adverbials *the verb is fucked*, it *can't express cause, means or comparison etc. with any degree of precision*
> without adverbials, memory is *no longer reliable*
> without adverbials, verbs will be *orphans* like him

In short, Moses argues that adverbials complete the verb, define the circumstances in which actions are taken, allow verbs to express their function with precision, and aid memory. Without adverbials, verbs are orphans, meaning they are without a home, which is why Moses loses them when he loses his home, meaning when the brothel is destroyed by the Mayor seeking re-election. In order to recover from this loss, Moses feels he needs to kill the Mayor, which he does. However, what is of more concern for us here is how this description of the function of adverbials in *Black Moses* can assist in both better understanding the manner in which sham ruins function and in developing a strategy for repurposing sham ruins into tools for change. The whole discussion of this chapter will center around the role of the home in literature and film, an important topic for a book on an architectural feature that rarely houses anyone (just the odd paid hermit or two), thus sham ruins are perfectly poised as objects with which a critique of house and home can be made.

Therefore, the first question that should be asked here is, with sham ruins, what functions as the verb and what as the adverbial? Are sham ruins one of these, or are they a force which separates one from the other, a force which orphans verbs, leaving them stranded from their context, kicking them out of their home?

As mentioned earlier, the function of sham ruins is rather contentious. Kenneth Clark argues that they exist "to stimulate the imagination" (46–7) and nothing more, while Lauren Kaplan calls sham ruins "exotic" because they are located neither in the past nor present (56–7). Much like Moses' memory becoming unreliable with the loss of adverbials, sham ruins are objects lost in time, not really a part of the past they pretend to be from, and purposely removed from any architectural styles of the present. This is what separates sham ruins from real ones, since actual ruins were once real, contemporary, functional buildings that only became ruins over time. Actual ruins are thus connected to truth, as seen in this often-quoted passage from Italian architect and theorist Aldo Rossi: "the fragment in architecture is very important since it may be that only ruins express a fact completely. Photographs of cities during war, sections of apartments, broken toys. Delphi and Olympia" (7). Yet if we continue with this quote, which is taken from Rossi's *A Scientific Autobiography*, we can see that he uses fragments, in a very postmodern sense, to address the whole: "This ability to use pieces of mechanisms whose overall sense is partly lost has always interested me, even in formal terms. I am thinking of a unity, or a system, made solely of reassembled fragments" (ibid.). Although sham ruins are not about fragments in the way Rossi is thinking, the loss of their overall sense both describes the way sham ruins are floating in time as well as how Moses becomes unmoored from temporality through the loss of his adverbials.

Yet does this help us decide what element sham ruins represent in Moses' adverbial trauma? Let's see. Adverbials help to situate a whole clause, to give it context, to provide it with a time and a place, to offer a home. Sham ruins do none of these things. No one really lives in them now, and no one ever did in the past. They are specifically objects which are outside of their context, which is one of the 'sham' elements of them. In other words, sham ruins are not just shams because they are not real ruins, but also because they are objects which are meant to look like they were made in a time, and sometimes even in a place, far removed from their actual construction. So in this way sham ruins are very much not adverbials. They are more like anti-adverbials. They are what is left over after adverbials are gone. Thus, we can now go back to *Black Moses* and see how the protagonist describes his feeling of being adverbialness to see what kind of clues can be picked up about the way sham ruins are.

One of the main effects on Moses when he loses his adverbials is that he loses direction. Without a job and doing little but tending his garden of spinach, Moses likes to go for walks. But without adverbials he starts to lose his way. To counter this, Moses comes up with a trick:

> Because I was going round and round in circles, like a snail caught in the spiral of its own slime, I needed some little trick for working out where I was when I went wandering. Using my stick, I drew a cross of Lorraine wherever I went, to avoid doubling back the same way a few minutes later.
>
> (Mabanckou 158)

His neighborhood eventually becomes full of crosses of Lorraine, although when some of the locals learn what he is doing, they start making their own marks so that Moses "couldn't tell my crosses of Lorraine from those of the jokers"; therefore, he gives up marking crosses and "spent my time rubbing them out instead" (ibid.).

Here, we have two elements so far developed regarding sham ruins and one new element. Regarding what has been previously developed, when Moses mixes up his real markers with those made by his joker neighbors, it is similar to how sham ruins become indistinguishable from real ones over the course of time. On the other hand, the use of crosses of Lorraine as the markers indicates some of the political uses for which sham ruins have been used. As David Stewart was shown to argue in the first chapter, sham ruins can function as "images of *just* destruction" (400), meaning that pretend medieval towers which are part of a preplanned ruin were actually a commentary on how the backward days of Catholicism had fallen to the present age of reason. In a similar manner, the cross of Lorraine, although it has a long history, has come to be associated with colonial France (Lawler). Thus, when Moses loses his way he attempts to find it by using a symbol of colonial France, a technique which eventually stops working.

Yet there is at least one more element to this scene in the novel, and one which has so far not been discussed in relation to sham ruins. Moses suggests a strategy of what to do next. In other words, rather than just describing the function (or lack thereof) of sham ruins, Moses shows what to do with them. This is seen in the final part of the quote previously, when Moses gives up his attempts at keeping track of where he walks and instead spends his time rubbing out all the crosses of Lorraine, both his own and those made by others. It is this rubbing out that will be the focus of the rest of the chapter since it offers a strategy, if a destructive and dangerous one, for using the strengths of sham ruins when one is faced with the oppressive monstrosity of real ones.

Therefore, we can now ask, what would it mean to rub out your home?

Let Me Just Destroy That for You

Francis Ford Coppola's film *The Conversation* (1974) offers one answer.

Harry Caul (Gene Hackman) is a private surveillance expert. At the end of the film, his client's assistant calls him to say that he no longer needs him to look into the case. In fact, the assistant insists on Caul's dropping the matter, saying "We'll be listening to you" as an open threat. This drives Caul, who makes his living from eavesdropping, to tear his own home apart in order to find any devices his client may have had planted. Caul rips up floorboards and digs into the walls until his home turns into a demolition zone. Then, in the end, Caul picks up his saxophone to play, seemingly resigned to having to live the rest of his life in what Shoshana Zuboff much later called the "age of surveillance capitalism" (Zuboff). Yet watching this scene in the context of sham ruins, we can see that what Caul actually does is merely turn his home into what it always already was: an unsecured place that could have always been tapped, just as Caul was doing to others. In other words, Caul's destruction merely turns his home into what it already was: not a ruin, but a sham ruin. His home would be a ruin if it had functioned, at one time, as a home, and then was turned into something else. Instead, from the beginning, this space was open to the surveillance of others (as all our homes are). From the start, his home was not really a home. The destruction he causes merely foregrounds the state his home had always occupied. It was never what he thought it was. Just as the homes of those he taps into only function as covers for his illicit surveillance.

Yet just as the function of sham ruins differs from one to the other, the destruction of homes in films does not always have the same role. In Michael Haneke's first feature film *The Seventh Continent* (1989), an Austrian middle-class family is shown going through the various aspects of their mundane lives. Then, after a visit to their grandparents, the father decides that the family is going to leave, presumably to the seventh continent of the film's title, meaning Australia. However, what happens instead is that the family methodically destroys their home, flushing their money down the toilet and smashing their fish tank, only to have the father kill each of them, as well as himself, in the end.

The destruction of home in *The Conversation* was related to the porousness of walls that are otherwise taken as solid. Walls do not start their lives as solid barriers to the outside world and then degrade into ruins, full of holes, through which the world is listening. Rather, Caul's destruction merely shows the way that all homes are already built in the style of easy listening. The family in *The Seventh Continent* destroys their home with a different purpose in mind. In no way is this film about surveillance (that would be reserved for the filmmaker's later film *Caché (2005)*). Instead, it is about family, and family institutions, and family norms, and family disappointments. In other words, the home in Haneke's film is also a sham ruin, but a different kind. From the beginning of the film, when the family is shown just going about their everyday activities of eating breakfast and so on, the home is already dysfunctional, enclosing the family within forced, cold, emotionless situations. Thus, when D.I. Grossvogel argues that in this film, "Haneke set out to show how the daily repetitions of a trivialized existence lead ultimately to the rage that causes its victims to destroy their material possessions and ultimately themselves" (36), he misses a beat in that it is not the daily repetitions of trivialized existence that lead to rage but rather another force which lies behind these repetitions. Thus, the house, in this film, is not just a house, but rather an instigator of family obligations, expectations, mortgages, and the pressure to keeps jobs one does not love. The house is already a sham even before it is destroyed because it never does the work that it is expected to do. It does not bring the family together; it tears them apart. Thus, taking the home apart, piece-by-piece, merely exposes the domestic structure for what it is: a sham.

And yet another kind of house destruction is involved in Jean-Marc Vallée's film *Demolition* (2015). One night when Davis (Jake Gyllenhall) and his wife Julia (Heather Lind) are driving home they are hit by another car and Julia dies. After recovering from his injuries, Davis realizes that he never actually loved Julia. During the time that Julia's parents insist on creating a foundation to award an annual scholarship in Julia's name, Davis learns that she was unfaithful to him and had become pregnant with another man's child. Davis responds to all of this with very little emotion. However, as the title of the film indicates, he begins to demolish, from the inside, the expensive, modern home that they shared together. First, attacking the kitchen appliances, and then his computer, eventually Davis gets a bulldozer and, with the help of a friend, levels the house to the ground.

The demolition in Vallée's film takes on a much more personal nature than that found in either *The Conversation* or *The Seventh Continent*. Yet Davis' demolition has a similar effect. Taking apart his home, first slow and then fast, merely shows the home for what it always was: a sham. This destruction does not turn a solid home into a ruin; rather, it shows that the home was always a ruin, that it was broken, just like his marriage, from the start, and in that sense, even though its appearance is a fully functioning home, its function is that of a fake. It just takes its destruction to bring its true face into the light.[2]

When we take the different home deconstructions so far presented in this chapter together, we start to see a common denominator. Moses's loss of adverbials which accompanied his loss of home when the brothel was destroyed, Caul's taking his apartment apart piece-by-piece to find any hidden surveillance devices, Haneke's family destroying their home just as their sense of family had already been destroyed, and Davis' dismantling of his marriage being mirrored in the demolition of his home all share a strategy of dismantling an object in order to show that it never really functioned the way it was intended. In other words, objects, such as a home, are broken back to their state of original brokenness. Flashy veneers are gone. An object's true function is represented in its appearance, rather than being hidden behind a flashy facade. Thus, the films show that sham ruins are real ruins, while actual ruins are fake. This is because sham ruins are ruins from the start, while 'actual' ruins do not start out as ruins but as something else and only gradually become ruins over time.

Punking Objects

The work this chapter has done so far is to show sham ruins for what they truly are. Yet a certain process needed to be engaged in order to do this. One name for this process is destruction. The name given in the next part of this chapter is 'punking objects,' and the sub-genre of salvagepunk is used to develop this idea. While salvagepunk is initially seen as a genre of *construction* out of the ruins, with the example of Miguel Llansó's film *Crumbs* (2015) we will see that the genre is really about showing the already-existing sham nature of objects, even when this sham nature is hidden.

The term *salvagepunk* was coined by Evan Calder Williams to gather together science fiction literature and film with a ruined agenda. The genre takes place in "a world of stealing from the ruins, robbing the graves, and rearranging the leftovers" (70). The key feature of salvagepunk is that instead of reimagining objects as something different from what they are, actually existing objects are punked into something new. This was seen previously in how the homes in different films were not turned into other objects (a store or a bank, for example), but rather were destroyed into something else. Yet Williams sees salvagepunk not as a genre of demolition, but as constructing something new out of debris. He argues that it is about "choice and construction" (ibid.) rather than reimagination and rehistorization. This construction takes place by means of what I call 'punking objects,' meaning – in the words of Virginie Despentes, "The whole point of punk is not doing what you're told to do" (110). While sham ruins are objects which are ruined from the beginning, punking objects will be seen as a technique of bringing out the hidden sham nature of many of the unseen ruins around us.

Punk sometimes gets a bad name, especially when considered a mere stylistic disruption, one more interested in safety pins and spiked hair than systematic, global change. But this is not the only kind of punk there is. Punks are also great recyclers, turning safety pins and dog collars into what they were never meant to be. As Richard Hell says, punk is the opposite of the authentic use of things: "Punk is pretty funny. It's like reality itself, as exemplified by the statement, 'This sentence is a lie.' It's hard to be authentic" (99). Salvagepunk inauthenticizes objects, turning them away from their intended purpose toward something else. It creates the 'hostile objects' that were mentioned in the first chapter, which are "weirdly incommensurable with the purpose for which they were designed" (Williams 21). This is more than just a question of style. As key salvagepunk works found later suggest, punking objects into something new might lead to something better.

China Miéville's novel *Perdido Street Station* (2000) is a key reference for salvagepunk (Willems 105–6). In part, the novel tells the story of Isaac, a scientist who accidentally grows a strange caterpillar into a deadly monster, called a slake moth, which ends up feeding on the minds of its victims. In order to fight them, Isaac enlists the help of the Construct Council – a giant formed out of junk from a garbage dump, a collection of repurposed salvage: "The rubbish was a body. A vast skeleton of industrial waste twenty-five feet from skull to toe" (Miéville 547). Yet the novel also inserts a new element into the concept of salvagepunk, and thus into sham ruins. The "repurposing, détourning, and scrapping" (Williams 20) of salvagepunk is not initiated by a human hand; rather it is caused by nonhuman agents. New objects are the product of forces outside of human control, "thrown together and powered without the intervention of human design" (Miéville 548). This calls to mind a passage from Jane Bennett's *Vibrant Matter* in which a number of discarded objects are punked into life. A glove, pollen, a dead rat, a bottle cap, and a stick of wood are not just junk lying in the street; they have an effect on the viewer, and they are a group of objects "that commanded attention in its own right, as existents in excess of their association with human meanings, habits, or projects" (4). Salvagepunk is not just about objects used by humans in new *human* ways, but it features objects with new functions that lie outside the human context. This is also what saves salvagepunk from simply being style: non-human organizations of knowledge and functions can lead to a kind of freedom away from the limitations and damage of human understanding and action (Brassier).

Non-human organizations are important because we are living in a devastated world brought about by our own hubris. And the world needs to get punked. The irreversible ecological collapse of the Anthropocene indicates how the destruction of humanity has become a "global geophysical force" (Steffen, Crutzen and McNeill 614), and neoliberalism has become so pervasive that it seems impossible to imagine any alternative (Jameson 76). The world is not heading for an apocalypse; the apocalypse has already happened. As Williams puts it, "the world is now irrevocably structured as apocalyptic wasteland" (36). Salvagepunk is the proper genre for the current age because it not only says that the world has "*already been burnt, already lost at sea*" (ibid.) but also shows how "we can only begin again from here if we finish wrecking – in thought – what we know to be wreckage yet which refuses to call itself such" (36–7). Or, as Miéville says in an interview, "It's too late to *save*, but we might repurpose" (Miéville).

Sham ruins are all about repurposing. This is why the ironic subtitle of this book, *A User's Guide*, indicates the usability of an object which is specifically designed not to work, but just to be a showpiece. The multiple manners that these objects of style are used, whether political, artistic, or otherwise, is the focus of this book. Salvagepunk takes on a similar role in that it focuses on the manner that debris, which are objects which have worn out their use, become repurposed as other things. Yet in the context of sham ruins we can see that these objects, even before they were thrown away, always are debris, and thus have always had the potential for these 'other' purposes. That is what makes them sham ruins, and it is also what connects salvagepunk to the next piece of work under discussion.

Crumbs

In Llansó's film *Crumbs*, Candy (Daniel Tadesse) and his fiancée Birdy (Selam Tesfayie) exist in a post-apocalyptic Ethiopia (filmed in the northern region of Dallol) in which the remaining pop-cultural objects from our time take on new meaning. A short plastic Christmas tree is worth risking your life for; a plastic sword, still cable-tied to its packaging, becomes a defensive weapon; and a vinyl copy of Michael Jackson's 1991 album *Dangerous* pays for a wedding. Although these objects are all products of industrial technology, they are not the technological fetishes of cyberpunk. Nor are they the re-crafted Victoriana of steampunk. Instead, these objects show how Candy and Birdy are "stealing from the ruins, robbing the graves" (Williams 70) of their past, of our own present. As Mark Bould, who has also connected *Crumbs* and salvagepunk, says of the film, "There is the detritus of a lost world, given fresh meaning" (Bould). Objects are not given new history or imagined as something else but rather are found to already contain the potential for constructing new theories and values. As Miéville says, salvagepunk is about "tinkering in broken crap with aggressive uninterest in original usages" (Miéville). This is the repurposing energy of punk at work, doing with objects what they were not meant to do. As Llansó has said:

> For me punk is not a music style but it's more linked to the subversion of genres and the freewheeling creative force. In this sense (politically and aesthetically) punk is an-archist, because it destroys the "arch" (*arché* in ancient Greek means "principles," "dogmas," "grounds," so anarchism means lack of grounds or dogmas). So basically punk is the invention of new rules, getting rid of the old ones.
>
> (Llansó)

In *Crumbs*, freedom does not only mean that objects can take on new economic value. There is also a spiritual dimension. Michael Jordan has become a god, as have Just Bieber IV and San Pablo Picasso. The film features objects which now signify new things because their meanings follow different rules. This is done by taking these objects out of their everyday human contexts. The removal from this context is represented by periodic shots of these objects slowly rotating in space above Earth, far away from any human contact.

Thus, the film indicates that there is something other than human involved in punking objects. Previously, I argued that in the age of the Anthropocene, when human influence is measured on a global scale, non-human organizations of knowledge are necessary to invent new rules which are different from those that devastated the planet. *Crumbs* represents this not only by punking objects but also by punking the human through the figure of Candy. Thus, it falls into line with science fiction that engages in what I have called "the Zug Effect," the name of which I take from Damon Knight's 1964 novel *Beyond the Barrier*, in which a human who is sent out to kill an alien Zug finds out he was the monster all along (Willems 14–30; Knight 133). The Zug Effect, I have argued, is found whenever an object displays qualities or functions that cannot be subsumed into any past, present, or future orders of human knowledge. It is a name for the incommensurably alien. A contemporary iteration of the Zug Effect can be found in Nnedi Okorafor's *Binti (2015–18)* trilogy, in which Binti slowly learns that the real strangeness in her life is located inside herself, as she has been unknowingly carrying alien DNA. Thus, when she asks the punk-ish question "Why don't I ever want to do what I'm supposed to do?" (Okorafor 132), we can also read this as the vocalization of a sham ruin, which never functions in the manner it is supposed to. Sham ruins are made that way from the start.

Punking expectations is scary because it leads to new objects, to new people. As Jameson argues, there is "a thoroughgoing anxiety in the face of everything we stand to lose in the course of so momentous a transformation that – even in the imagination – it can be thought to leave little intact of current passions, habits, practices, and values" (Jameson 60). The non-human punking of objects can be frightening, because it indicates new rules to follow, new directions to go, new ways of being. This is also the strength of punk, of its "freewheeling creative force," in the words of Llansó. The specificity of salvagepunk is that it can find this creative force in the detritus of the apocalypse of the present.

Yet in Llansó's film it is the objects of pop culture that are punked, and they are punked by being pulled out of the time of their original production and reception and put in another. This relates to the loss of time that accompanied the loss of adverbials in *Black Moses*. However, Mabanckou's novel indicated a loss of not only time but also space. The loss of space is important in the next section. For what would it look like to really create a modern sham ruin in the form of a home, meaning, creating, from scratch, a house that was never meant to function at all? This would not be a temporally punked piece of debris but rather an object whose spatial coordinates are punk from the get-go. What kind of reactions would such a construction cause? What new forms would it be found to have? These are some of the questions engendered by the last work under discussion in this book, Ivan Vladislavić's *The Folly* (1993).

The Folly, a Conclusion

Reading Vladislavić's novel about the purposeful construction of a non-functioning home was one of the main reasons I started thinking about sham ruins, so it is a fitting end to this book to return to the text and see how it relates to the thought of sham ruins developed.

A man named Nieuwenhuizen suddenly appears on an empty lot located in a residential area somewhere in South Africa, near the time of the fall of apartheid. The name 'Nieuwenhuizen' of course means 'new house,' and building a new house is exactly what this man begins to do. However, the house he builds is not a functioning dwelling made of bricks and mortar, but rather a useless sham constructed out of string and imagination. Watching all of this are the neighbors, only referred to as Mr and Mrs Malgas, the former of which gets involved in the house's construction, while the latter merely worries about the former. Thus, amid nightly news stories of violence and unrest, including the destruction of the shanty townhomes of oppressed blacks, Nieuwenhuizen constructs his own sham ruin, thereby showing how the space of the home has an allegorical function in the way, in the words of the author, the "political system gets reflected in the physical space and how the space, in turn, shapes the kinds of social relations that are possible" (Kitamura and Vladislavić 73).

At first, Nieuwenhuizen seems to approach his home in the mode of salvagepunk, seeing an old oil drum "brim-full of potential" (Vladislavić 12), using a broken bottle to dig a moat (21), and turning an old FOR SALE sign, which "had useful object written all over it" (22) into a braai-grille (23). Yet if this were the only approach to home in the novel, there would be no reason to include it here, since it adds very little not already covered.

Yet Nieuwenhuizen's new house is not made out of the discarded refuse that he finds on his lot. In fact, he specifically wants to build a new, non-functioning domicile. His old house was a ruin: a good house that then deteriorated: "it had served its time. It was falling apart" (34). A new house is needed, but one which does not function, at least not in any traditional way, from the start.

First, he divides his land into a grid, numbering the squares. Then, he gets Mr Malgas, who works in a hardware store, to obtain 300 new, very specific nails: they are larger, like the kind they use for railroad tracks (83–4). The nails then are driven into the ground all across the grid, but when Nieuwenhuizen takes a ball of string and ties it to one nail, and then uses it to go from nail to nail to start mapping out the plan of the house, something strange starts happening. Once any recognizable part of the house is formed, it just as soon gets crossed out, negated:

> Nieuwenhuizen went from nail to nail, stooping and looping. From time to time, when he stood back to observe the emerging plan, Mr Malgas studied it too, climbing up on his stool and peeping from under the pelmet in the hope that added elevation would bring greater insight. Nothing worthy of being called a new house suggested itself, neither rising above the ground nor sinking below. Something resembling a room would appear, a string-bound rectangle of the appropriate dimensions, but soon enough Nieuwenhuizen would put a cross through it, or deface it with a diagonal. By some stretch of the imagination a passage would become viable, only to be obliterated a moment later by a drunken zigzag. An unmistakable corner, a perfect right angle, survived for close on an hour. Mr Malgas became convinced that it was the extremity of the rumpus room Nieuwenhuizen had once referred to. But, without blinking, Nieuwenhuizen allowed it to spin out an ugly slash that traversed the entire plan and dislocated every element of it.
>
> (117–18)

Every time Mr Maglas thought a room was coming into shape, maybe a bathroom or part of the kitchen, "Nieuwenhuizen backed into it in his big boots, unreeling his string, and crossed it off the plan" (118). There is a concerted effort here in building a new house, but a new house that in the process of being built cancels out its own function. This is not an error, not a mistake in materials, blueprints, or skill. It is intentional. When a function of the house starts to become apparent, Nieuwenhuizen ruins it. And when the construction is done, Nieuwenhuizen asks Mr Maglas to see, really to see, what they had constructed together, but Mr Maglas merely:

> found himself in the midst of an immense, tattered net full of holes and knots and twisted threads, more holes than threads. . . . It was a shambles. It was so unremittingly drunken and disorderly that tears started from Maglas's eyes.
>
> (121–2)

This house is a spatial ruin, from the start.

Yet this does not mean the house does not have a function. Nieuwenhuizen is not just creating a mess. He can see a house and lives in a house, and eventually Mr Maglas can see it too. But it is not easy. First, he does not see it, but when Nieuwenhuizen spends some days just sleeping in his tent, Mr Maglas takes over the role of caretaker and begins to lubricate the nails to protect them from rust and oiling the string with dubbin and beeswax to protect it (131). Mr Maglas still does not see the house that Nieuwenhuizen does, but he goes through the motions anyway of taking care, and it is through those actions, emptied of faith and containing merely rote ritual, that Mr Maglas first sees a keystone, and then, 2 days later, a balustrade floats into view (134). From then on, Mr Maglas is able to see the house in all of its details just as Nieuwenhuizen can, although to everyone else it is just a jumble of string and a pile of garbage.

Eventually, the sham home is dismantled, and Nieuwenhuizen goes on his way. However, Vladislavić's novel foregrounds one of the essential points developed in this text for the use of unusable objects. In first repurposing garbage (such as using a broken bottle as a shovel) and then abandoning this repurposing for a different house-building technique, the novel shows how sham ruins are not ruined objects, like waste, but rather objects which themselves ruin something. This ruination is one of the keys to understanding how sham ruins 'work.' At the same time, it is not important what sham ruins ruin exactly, but rather that they are able to ruin. However, through the use of all of the examples in this book, a commonality to sham ruins' targets can be found. What sham ruins ruin is what an object is not. They take aim at some of the assumptions made about how things work. The destruction of houses shows how houses are not really the homes they were taken for. *First on the Moon* shows it was not really the documentary that at least some people assumed it was. And the art of Sturtevant indicates that the art of the original artists was involved in a much larger network of production, reception, and exhibition than was assumed at first.

Thus, it is only when something is purposely broken that its true function can be revealed. Everything else is just a sham.

Notes

1. Lynn Nottage's play *Ruined* (2007) also features a kind of brothel-as-home in Congo, although it is set in the early twenty-first century and the brother is a more problematic refuge. In Mabanckou's earlier novel *African Psycho* (2003), a similar orphan-turned criminal takes center stage, although this one is intent on murder, and thus his encounter with sex workers is either one of mere physical relief or violent thoughts of rape and murder.
2. Near the end of the film, it might seem that Davis reconciles with his wife's affair when he agrees to help her parents restore an old carousel. However, in the final

scene, Davis is seen watching the demolition of some high rises, denoting that his propensity for destruction has not faded one bit.

Works Cited

Bennett, Jane. *Vibrant Matter: A Political Ecology of Things*. Durham: Duke University Press, 2010.

Bould, Mark. "*Crumbs* (Miguel Llansó, Ethiopia/Spain/Finland, 2015)." *Markbould.com* (Nov 18, 2015). Internet: https://markbould.com/2015/11/18/crumbs-miguel-llanso-ethiopiaspainfinland-2015/.

Brassier, Ray. "Unfree Improvisation/Compulsive Freedom." *Mattin.org* (2013). Internet: www.mattin.org/essays/unfree_improvisation-compulsive_freedom.html.

Clark, Kenneth. *The Gothic Revival: An Essay in the History of Taste*. New York: Harper & Row, 1972.

Despentes, Virginie. *King Kong Theory*. Trans. Stéphanie Benson. New York: Feminist Press, 2010.

Grossvogel, D.I. "The Coercing of Vision." *Film Quarterly*, Vol. 60, No. 4 (Summer 2007): 36–43.

Hell, Richard. *Massive Pissed Love: Nonfiction 2001–2014*. Berkeley: Soft Skull Press, 2015.

Jameson, Fredric. "Future City." *New Left Review*, Vol. 21 (2003): 65–79.

Jameson, Fredric. *The Seeds of Time*. New York: Columbia University Press, 1996.

Kaplan, Lauren. "Exotic Follies: Sanderson Miller's Mock Ruins." *Frame*, Vol. 1 (Spring 2011): 54–68.

Kitamura, Katie and Ivan Vladislavić. "Ivan Vladislavić." *BOMB*, No. 135 (2016): 72–8.

Knight, Damon. *Beyond the Barrier*. New York: Macfadden-Bartell, 1970.

Lawler, Nancy. "The Crossing of the Gyaman to the Cross of Lorraine: Wartime Politics in West Africa, 1941–1942." *African Affairs*, Vol. 96, No. 382 (1997): 53–71.

Llansó, Miguel. Message to author (Apr 16, 2018). E-mail.

Mabanckou, Alain. *African Psycho*. London: Serpent's Tail, 2009.

Mabanckou, Alain. *Black Moses*. London: Serpent's Tail, 2017.

Miéville, China. *Perdido Street Station*. London: Pan Books, 2000.

Miéville, China. "Problems of Salvage. 1: Ancestral Shame." *Rejectamentalist Manifesto* (Aug 2, 2010). Internet: http://chinamieville.net/post/892894355/problems-of-salvage-1-ancestral-shame.

Miéville, China. "A Strategy for Ruination." *Boston Review* (Jan 8, 2018). Internet: http://bostonreview.net/literature-culture-china-mieville-strategy-ruination.

Nottage, Lynn. *Ruined*. New York: Theater Communications Group, 2009.

Okorafor, Nnedi. *Binti: Home*. New York: TOR, 2017.

Rossi, Aldo. *A Scientific Autobiography*. Cambridge: MIT Press, 1981.

Steffen, Will, Paul Crutzen and John McNeill. "The Anthropocene: Are Humans Now Overwhelming the Great Forces of Nature?" *Ambio*, Vol. 36, No. 8 (2007): 614–21.

Stewart, David. "Political Ruins: Gothic Sham Ruins and the '45." *Journal of the Society of Architectural Historians*, Vol. 55, No. 4 (Dec 1996): 400–11.

Thompson, Sandra, Robert Longacre and Shin Ja Hwang. "Adverbial Clauses." In *Language Typology and Syntactic Description, Volume II: Complex Constructions*. Ed. Timothy Shopen. Cambridge: Cambridge University Press, 2007: 237–300.

Vladislavić, Ivan. *The Folly*. Brooklyn: Archipelago Books, 2015.

Willems, Brian. *Speculative Realism and Science Fiction*. Edinburgh: University of Edinburgh Press, 2017.

Williams, Evan Calder. *Combined and Uneven Apocalypse: Luciferian Marxism*. Hants: Zero Books, 2010.

Williams, Evan Calder. "Hostile Object Theory." In *Spooky Action: A Materialist Nightmare*. Ed. Patricia Margarita Hernandez. Miami: [Name] Publications, 2016: 18–40.

Zuboff, Shoshana. *The Age of Surveillance Capitalism: The Fight for a Human Future at the New Frontier of Power*. London: Profile Books, 2019.

Index

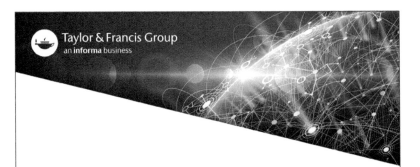

For Product Safety Concerns and Information please contact our EU representative GPSR@taylorandfrancis.com Taylor & Francis Verlag GmbH, Kaufingerstraße 24, 80331 München, Germany

Batch number: 08153772

Printed by Printforce, the Netherlands